The Church in Mission

William J. Martin

GOSPEL PUBLISHING HOUSE
SPRINGFIELD, MISSOURI

02-0803

Unless otherwise indicated, all Scripture quotations are taken from the HOLY BIBLE: NEW INTERNATIONAL VERSION. Copyright ©1978 by the New International Bible Society. Used by permission of Zondervan Bible Publishers.

©1986 by Gospel Publishing House, Springfield, Missouri 65802. All rights reserved. No part of this book may be reproduced, stored in a retrieval system, or transmitted in any form or by any means—electronic, mechanical, photocopy, recording, or otherwise—without prior written permission of the copyright owner.

This is a Sunday School Staff Training textbook. Credit for its study will be issued under Classification 3, Sunday School Department, Assemblies of God.

Library of Congress Catalog Card Number 86-80022
International Standard Book Number 0-88243-803-4
Printed in the United States of America

Contents

Foreword 5
Introduction 7
 1. Meaning and Mission 9
 2. Sunday School and Mission 22
 3. Laity and Mission 34
 4. Preparing People for Mission 47
 5. Witness and Mission 59
 6. Doctrine and Mission 70
 7. Worship and Mission 82
 8. Fellowship and Mission 94
 9. Leadership and Mission 107
10. Method and Mission 119

Foreword

The Church in Mission is a masterly study of what our Lord desires of His church with regard to the Great Commission.

Evangelism and Christian education are inseparable. Worship and training go hand in hand. Christian education—nurture in the faith—leads to evangelism, and evangelism leads to nurture.

The author clearly charts our Lord's plan. Converts are to affiliate and identify with the body of Christ. This is to be followed by their being discipled and then, in turn, winning others.

I have found the 10 chapters to be personally helpful. The author shows the important place of the Sunday school in providing opportunities for teaching and equipping the body of Christ for ministry.

From the opening chapter on meaning and mission, William J. Martin discusses the role of laity and clergy and the importance of preparation. Chapters are given to witnessing, doctrine, fellowship, leadership, and methods.

Here is a book for every minister and devout Christian. It gives us the connection and sequence in Christian education and evangelism that we need to see—and follow.

G. RAYMOND CARLSON
GENERAL SUPERINTENDENT
ASSEMBLIES OF GOD

Introduction

For a long time I have wanted to write about the church in mission. However, having written this book, I feel a sense of inadequacy because I realize that to properly define and consider the subject of the church's mission requires volumes.

What this book does more than anything else is place some issues on the table for discussion. My prayer is that the discussion will lead to action, and action will increase the church's obedience to mission.

To gain a comprehensive view of the church in mission, I would encourage the reader to consider three books as a trilogy related to this subject.

Teaching To Meet Crisis Needs, by Dr. Billie Davis, deals with the Sunday school as a primary center for helping people. It eloquently reminds us that Sunday schools are a natural center for doing many of the things included in the mission of the church.

Equipping for Ministry, by John Palmer, deals with training laity for service.[1] It offers strategies for training every believer as a minister.

This book, *The Church in Mission,* considers the purpose of the church and establishes the rationale for helping and equipping people.

In her book, Dr. Davis quoted a study from the University of Nebraska which dealt with burnout. The researchers concluded that to prevent burnout and be successful in any people-helping vocation (of which Christian ministry is an expression), three things must be present: a sense of mission (purpose), empathy, and proficiency. Using these three things, I would suggest a parallel with the books mentioned:

Proficiency is considered in *Equipping for Ministry.*
Empathy is considered in *Teaching To Meet Crisis Needs.*
Purpose is considered in *The Church in Mission.*

Understanding what these books teach will help the reader recognize a great truth: From its inception, the Sunday school has been, and continues to be, a primary center for accomplishing God's will in the lives of believers.

---

[1] *Teaching To Meet Crisis Needs* (02-0609) and *Equipping for Ministry* (02-0802) are available from Gospel Publishing House.

1
Meaning and Mission

The situation is familiar to most of us. An average church finds its needs intensifying and its ministries proliferating as it experiences growth. It is faced with the increasing task of reaching out to those both inside and outside the congregation.

The church leadership meets to consider the situation. They soon identify the number one problem—lack of involved, committed people. There are not enough volunteers to sustain the growing ministries of the church.

As the leadership wrestles with the problem, some very familiar questions arise. Why aren't more people involved? Why is the core group so small? What can be done to excite and motivate people? Why is there so much apathy in the congregation?

Most churches fit this description at some point in their history. We want to consider why this is so, and what can be done when it occurs.

This book is written to help people understand what it means to be a Christian and why they are important in the plan of God. It is a book about purpose and mission, meaning and fulfillment in life.

For the church to be a dynamic center of God's work on this earth, the people of God must discover, understand, and accomplish the mission to which they have been called. As we discuss our mission, maybe we can also help churches like the one mentioned above.

The Contemporary Struggle for Meaning

The quest for personal meaning in life is one of the great

pursuits of mankind. This is especially true in modernized countries where creature comforts are plentiful, but lack of meaning is epidemic.

According to David Watson, "In our meaningless world, increasing numbers of people are looking for something to live for, perhaps even to die for. Why are the cults increasing in numbers, when the established churches are declining? The cults call for total commitment! So do the revolutionary and terrorist groups that are capturing so much of the world today."[1]

Sociologists, psychologists, and clergy point to many indicators of the mass lack of meaning people experience today. Consider three trends that reflect the search for meaning.

The first is the large number of teenagers either attempting or committing suicide. Some statisticians record suicide as the second leading cause of death for that age-group, following accidents. Still others suggest that it is the number one killer since many accidents are probably suicides in disguise.

The problem is tragic in human terms, but it relates to the theme of this book. Why are so many teens attempting or committing suicide? The experts seek to analyze and explain the problem. However, the church recognizes that many teens feel a despondency and lack of meaning in their lives. Their inner being is empty, feeling no sense of purpose, worth, or contribution in life. It is ironic that many of these teens have so much, but lack the thing they need the most—meaning. Personal meaning is so important that its loss leads people to believe there is nothing to live for, and they often embark on paths of self-destruction of one kind or another. Teen suicides reflect this.

A second trend indicative of the lack of meaning is the male mid-life crisis. This often occurs when a man reaches a change point at about 40 years old. He looks back on the first half of his life and conducts an evaluation.

For many men, the experience is negative, as they see too few accomplishments, wasted time and efforts, and failure to reach personal goals or expectations. They feel they have missed something or have failed to make a significant contribution anywhere.

Psychologists suggest the male's ego—his sense of worth and self-respect—is tied closely to his vocation. If his job has been rewarding, the result is a sense of positive self-worth. However, if the job has not been satisfying, the individual may feel deprived, useless, or that he has wasted many valuable years. Those feelings intensify and push the man to extremes in an attempt to ensure that the last half of life has meaning and fulfillment. In our materialistic society, tied so closely to vocational success, the presence of the male mid-life crisis has led to emotional breakdowns, countless divorces, and family traumas.

The third trend pointing to the lack of meaning problem is the pressure on women to find vocational outlets outside the home. Working outside the home is not wrong; the fault occurs when women feel pressured to leave the home in order to feel self-worth. Society has created the false impression that women are useless and have no meaning unless they are paid. Worth is tied to money and that, in itself, is an anti-Christian idea. Yet, it is a prominent one.

Women feel embarrassed to admit they are homemakers, believing society views that as meaningless. In an attempt to compensate, people have tried to attach a monetary value to the work done in the home by women, but this tends to confirm the belief that meaning and money go together. The service rendered by the homemaker is beyond compensation, yet many women, accepting society's idea of meaning, turn to employment in the marketplace. It is not money these women seek; it is meaning and fulfillment.

This attitude has major implications for the church, which is the largest volunteer organization in the world. In a culture where worth is evaluated by pay, it becomes increasingly difficult to find enough volunteers, especially among women who have traditionally formed the majority of church volunteers. Volunteerism has been wounded by the attitude that worth is tied to pay.

These trends are not cited to bemoan despondent teenagers, condemn men in mid-life crises, or indict working women. They are offered as examples to help us understand that we live in a culture of people desperately seeking meaning in their personal lives. The irony is that this struggle for meaning has developed in the wealthiest, most intelligent society the world has ever known. Meaning in life is not tied to material things, but to an inner feeling about oneself.

In *Teaching To Meet Crisis Needs,* Dr. Billie Davis quotes educator Arthur Combs, who has written about mankind, "We are seekers and creators of meaning and the meanings we create determine the ways we behave."[2] It is meaning that determines how we act. For Christians to act as they should, they must be in touch with meaning in their lives.

Unfortunately, the church has suffered from enculturation, reflecting the society much more than it should. Much of the apparent apathy, the prejudice against "programs," and the struggle to recruit volunteers reflect the lack of personal meaning among Christians. That is why it is so important to consider the mission of the church given to us by Christ. Conforming to our mission results in meaning, and meaning motivates us to positive action.

Where's the Meaning?

Meaning in life comes when we begin to answer the *why* questions.

In society, there is always a struggle between the idealist and the pragmatist. The idealist is the dreamer. The pragmatist is the realist. The idealist is seen as one who engages only in ideas and theories. The pragmatist is considered to be a practitioner, one who gets things done. In our culture of rugged, self-made people, the pragmatic practitioners are often preferred and held in high esteem.

This struggle was much in evidence during the 1970s "back-to-the-basics" movement. The underlying assumptions of the movement included the belief that knowing *how to* do things was the greatest prize of all. However, the overemphasis on *how-to* worked against the one thing people sought the most—meaning.

How-to questions deal with the structures of life, the way things are done and their effectiveness. It is important to understand structures and methods, but that is not where transcendent meaning and fulfillment come from. What must be understood is that *how-to* questions mean little if the *why* questions are not answered first. *Why* questions deal with the quality and meaning of life. They force us to evaluate the quality of life and plan direction for our future.

We must acknowledge that this contrast is not meant to be either *how-to* or *why*. Rather, it's the sequence that counts. People need to know how to do things well. There is a certain satisfaction that comes from being a doer. The Bible encourages that. However, it is crucial to know *why* we are doing things.

People often see church programs as highly structured things to do that are expected and constant. If they don't understand how these programs fit into God's plan, people resist responsibility to them. Failure to explain why the programs are necessary results in apathy, prejudice, and stubborn aversion to involvement.

Why do people feel negative about doing things without understanding why? If we think back to our school days, most of us remember when a teacher asked us to do things for no apparent reason. We called it busywork. Doing it felt like a waste of time because we did not see the purpose. Busywork is a demoralizing activity and people resist it. Conducting church programs without explaining their purpose seems like busywork to a congregation.

On the other hand, people will rally to do some amazing and exhausting things when they can see how it fits into a larger, important scheme.

One of the buzzwords of contemporary America is *burnout*. Those who study burnout suggest that it can be caused by two things. In some cases, it is the result of overwork. People can work until they are physically, mentally, and emotionally depleted, with nothing else to give.

The other cause of burnout may be more prevalent. It is a feeling of alienation from one's task. When individuals feel that what they are doing does not fit or matter in the big picture of things around them, they become distracted, bored, uninterested, and they disengage from their task.

In the church, people burn out because they are doing *things* but cannot see how their service contributes to the goals and mission of the church. A teacher who is left to teach alone week after week in an out-of-the-way classroom without affirmation, attention, or encouragement will begin to feel detached and unappreciated. The next step is burnout.

All persons serving in the church must have a clear understanding of why they are doing their task and how it fits into the plans and mission of the church. Only then will they experience the meaning so necessary to motivate and sustain them.

Meaning comes from knowing why we are here, why we are serving, and why that is important in God's sight. Only after we have answered those questions will learning *how to* do things make sense.

The society in which we live is committed to teaching people to do things, yet people are crying to discover the *whys* of existence.

In *Teaching To Meet Crisis Needs,* Billie Davis suggests there are three things necessary for success among those in people-helping vocations. They are empathy, proficiency, and a sense of mission, or purpose. Empathy is being able to understand how others feel. That is important in order to respond at the need level. Proficiency relates to how well we prepare to do our job. A sense of mission motivates us and provides meaning. We can never perform as successfully as we should until we have a personal sense of mission. It is crucial that we embark on the journey to discover that mission. That is the major task of this book.

Let us consider what the mission of the church is and how

we can make it our personal mission as members of Christ's body.

The Christian Advantage

No way of living offers more potential for meaning and fulfillment in life than being a Christian. Jesus said, "I have come that they may have life, and have it to the full" (John 10:10). In Christ, we are to live life to the fullest extent. God has made us to experience life at its best. He wants every day to be meaningful. But we will achieve that only as we live according to His direction. What does that mean? God calls us into His kingdom and challenges us to accept His mission as our own. As we find our place in the plan of God, our lives take on their intended meaning.

Christians have the opportunity to live life so that it extends into eternity. In Him, the life we live now can have an impact forever.

All men and women live with a deep desire to perpetuate themselves, to live on in influence and memory long after they physically die. People want their lives to count for something, that is, to have transcendent meaning. Viktor Frankl, the Jewish psychiatrist and Holocaust survivor, wrote much about the Jews who lived through the Nazi prison camp experience. He concluded that those who survived did so because a personal reason to live motivated them. From those studies, Frankl felt that it was meaning that made us uniquely human. Man has a deep desire to make his life significant—he wants it to have purpose. That is a testimony to the fact that we are essentially spiritual creatures, looking to experience life at the spiritual level.

Material things do not provide meaning, but getting in touch with and becoming part of something far beyond ourselves adds a dimension of life that propels us. That is exactly what happens when we realize we are part of God's great plan for mankind.

The key to the thing we want most—meaning—is found in

understanding and participating in the mission of the church of Jesus Christ.

The Mission of the Church

Peter Wagner and his associates have developed seven vital signs for healthy, growing churches. The seventh is of interest for our discussion: Healthy, growing churches have their priorities straight. They recognize that the most important service they render is religious.

What does that mean? What are churches for? What do people expect of a church? Wagner writes:

> Dean Kelley, a sociologist of religion who works not for conservative churches but for the National Council of Churches in New York City, comes through loud and clear. In his opinion, the one indispensable function of the church in America is to explain the meaning of life to people in ultimate terms.[3]

He goes on to point out that people are seeking many things: food, employment, housing, security, health, stable marriages, God, and more. Wagner suggests that the church can to some degree help meet all those needs. But there is one that *only* churches can meet. He defines that as "the desire to know God personally." In plainer Biblical language, "Churches are places where people can be saved."

Churches have a unique mission in this world. It is the same as God's purpose for mankind. To understand the implications of that truth, we must consider the Biblical basis for our mission.

That is perfectly proper in a Sunday school training book because the Bible is our foundational curriculum. It is our standard of faith and practice. What does God's Word tell us about our mission?

We are first of all the people of God, the body of Christ. As such, we are called out by God from the world for a very specific purpose.

It is important that we see ourselves as a *people*. The book *Equipping for Ministry,* dealing with the subject of giftedness, makes the point well. John Palmer writes about the discovery he made as a pastor: "The greatest untapped source of potential ministers was sitting in the pews every Sunday morning."[4]

In the February 3, 1984, issue of *Christianity Today,* Dr. Robert Johnson wrote an article titled "What Is the Major Shift in Theological Focus?" He pointed out that the 1950s was the decade of emphasis on Christology. The 1960s emphasized God the Father and the nature of the Church. The 1970s focused on the nature and ministry of the Holy Spirit. It is Johnson's conviction that the theological thrust of the 1980s is on God's people. We see this clearly in the ever-expanding emphasis on the laity and their role in Christ's kingdom.

The comments of Palmer and Johnson are but an indication of the revitalization of lay ministry. It is a recovery of what the Bible has always taught: The church is the people of God acting in concert to accomplish His mission.

God's purpose for this world is great and is the same for all people. For us to see it in such expansive terms is very difficult. We simply cannot comprehend all God is doing at any given moment. The way God's people get in touch with His mission is through the local church. A priority goal of any local church is to help each Christian understand and perform the mission Christ gave in the local context: at home, work, the grocery store, laundry, shopping mall, and so forth. The mission to which we are called is most real when expressed through the natural and normal affairs of our lives. The challenge is to mobilize people to accept this mission, realizing that deep meaning and fulfillment will follow.

Volumes have been written on the mission of the church. For the sake of our discussion, let us define the mission simply. Essentially, it has two parts: (1) We are here for God and (2) we are here for other people.

In that twofold definition of mission, we can identify four components: worship, discipleship, fellowship, and evangelism.

Each of these components affects our efforts on behalf of God and other people.

What does it mean to be "here for God"? First Peter 2:9,10 helps us understand this:

> You are a chosen people, a royal priesthood, a holy nation, a people belonging to God, that you may declare the praises of him who called you out of darkness into his wonderful light. Once you were not a people, but now you are the people of God; once you had not received mercy, but now you have received mercy.

As people belonging to God, we have a responsibility to declare His praises. That sounds so obvious that it may come as a surprise, yet it is a foundation of our identity as Christians. This is the worship component of our mission, and the Bible continually calls God's people to make this a priority in life.

Worshiping God becomes the great purpose of our lives out of which everything else flows. And, as we will consider in chapter 7, worship is something we must teach and learn.

If we do not understand our purpose of worshiping God, then our mission to serve others will be hollow or little more than human altruism. Richard Foster, writing in *Celebration of Discipline,* boldly states that serving, without first worshiping, is a form of idolatry. Worshiping God gives our service its meaning. It defines why we serve (which is the how-to of Christian living). Worshiping God is our first mission in life as Christians.[5]

What does it mean to be "here for other people"? If worshiping is the foundation of our mission, then the building that rises on that foundation is service. Jesus is our example. He gave priority attention to worshiping God, and He went about doing good things for people. By His own admission, "The Son of Man did not come to be served, but to serve, and to give his life as a ransom for many" (Mark 10:45). His life was a living example of that truth.

Furthermore, Jesus called His followers to do the same (John 13:1-17). Christians are called to give priority attention to serving others, both those inside the family of God and those outside. This part of our mission is described in the Great Commission (Matthew 28:19,20). Notice carefully what Jesus had in mind as He outlined to His disciples the mission they were to accomplish. He asked them to do three things.

1. *Go and make disciples of all nations.* There is no greater service we can render to the cause of Christ than to share the gospel with those who do not know Him. Until every person has heard and had an opportunity to respond our mission is incomplete.

2. *Baptize them.* Baptism is the public symbol of incorporation into the body of Christ. It is a sign to the world that we belong to Jesus. Therefore, our mission is not complete until we help those who accept Christ become part of a local church.

3. *Teach them to obey everything I have commanded you.* Once people have become part of the local church, they are to be taught and trained to function as committed disciples. That means they must have the church's mission explained to them. They must begin to accomplish it in their own lives in order to have meaning as Christians. They must be taught what Jesus expects of them.

Our efforts to take the gospel to the world, whether by sharing the message or by helping those in need, comprise the outreach component of our mission.

The mission to be here for others includes more than taking the gospel to the world. It also includes relating to our brothers and sisters in Christ. A great deal of the New Testament specifically deals with the quality of our relationships in the body of Christ. We are a unique people, called to love and care for one another as an expression of our discipleship (John 13:34,35). This is the fellowship component of our mission.

In scriptural terms, it is as we unselfishly give ourselves in the service of God and others that we discover who we are and our self-worth. As we perform the mission of worshiping God and serving others, we begin to have meaning and fulfillment. We then become motivated for service.

What we must recognize is that discovering and fulfilling

this mission does not happen by accident. It is learned behavior. It is the result of the unique cooperation between the church and the Holy Spirit. That requires the discipleship component of our mission.

In church we are taught about our mission and given opportunity to involve ourselves. That is why we have Sunday school and other Christian education ministries. They form the discipleship arm of the church. They become the primary means for unfolding the mission to God's people.

In a real sense this entire book speaks to the discipleship component of our mission. We might explain it this way: As we give ourselves in worship to God, we are motivated to prepare ourselves to reach out in service and fellowship to others. That statement explains the twofold mission of the church and includes the four components that aid us in accomplishing our mission.

They are ambitious goals. But we can accomplish them because the Holy Spirit provides whatever we lack to fulfill our mission. He provides illumination, enablement, and guidance. He is the Comforter. That word comes from two Latin words, *con* and *forte,* meaning "with power." The Spirit comes to empower us for our mission.

People of all ages can be trained about the mission, mobilized for service, and sent out to accomplish their task. The Sunday school plays a critical role in the effort. The better the Sunday school functions, the more Christians are going to discover what God has planned for their lives. The result will be Christians who have a deep sense of commitment, meaning, and fulfillment.

NOTES

[1]David Watson, *Called and Committed* (Wheaton, IL: Harold Shaw Publishers, 1982), p. 44.

[2]Billie Davis, *Teaching To Meet Crisis Needs* (Springfield, MO: Gospel Publishing House, 1984), p. 21.

[3]C. Peter Wagner, *Your Church Can Grow* (Ventura, CA: Regal Books, 1979), p. 173.

[4]John Palmer, *Equipping for Ministry* (Springfield, MO: Gospel Publishing House, 1985), p. 6.

[5]Richard J. Foster, *Celebration of Discipline* (San Francisco: Harper & Row Publishers, 1978), p. 148.

2
Sunday School and Mission

If meaning is what God wants each of us to experience, and if He has designed life so that we can achieve it by (1) worshiping Him and (2) serving others, we must do all we can to see that truth taught and modeled in the church.

One of the great values of Billie Davis' book, *Teaching To Meet Crisis Needs,* is her point that the Sunday school "fits almost perfectly the description of a setting where human needs are met and problems can be solved."[1] She lists the Sunday school's advantages that help it minister to human needs, emphasizing the rediscovery of the potential and power of Sunday school.

We can take her point one step further. The Sunday school also serves as a primary center for teaching, learning, and participating in the twofold mission of the church as described in chapter 1.

When Robert Raikes responded to needy children by providing for them what was to become Sunday school, he was reaching out to people in crisis. But, in theological terms, he was also fulfilling his part of the church's mission. He was serving others. That, in fact, was his primary intent. He responded to what he believed to be God's purpose for his life. Thus, Sunday school also had its origination as an expression of the church's mission. That has not changed, although we sometimes express Sunday school inadequately or redefine it apart from its original purpose.

Teaching the Mission

Just as Dr. Davis reminds us that Sunday school is a major

tool for helping people, so it is also a primary center for teaching people about the church's mission.

Among the important mission-related truths taught best in Sunday school are

1. Every believer is called to mission.
2. Every believer should find deep meaning in fulfilling his part of the mission.
3. Every believer is important in God's great purpose for mankind.
4. Every believer can please God as he participates in the mission.
5. Every believer fulfills Biblical expectations when he participates in the mission.
6. Every believer can be trained for the mission.
7. The church can be the greatest facilitator for helping believers accomplish the mission.

Why is Sunday school so important as a center for teaching our mission? When conducted well, Sunday school is built around small groups called classes, making these groups significantly different from the large group attending worship services. That also identifies their value to the church. Things can happen in Sunday school classes that few other ministries allow.

First, people learn better in small groups if the leader/teacher is willing to let the small group function as it should. The teacher should refrain from dominating the class with a lecture, preferring instead open discussion, questions, and personal investigation.

Learning occurs best in an atmosphere of open interaction. This is often called involvement learning. When people are allowed to participate in their own learning, they are mentally engaged, alert, and retain information longer. They receive strength from a growing support group as they live out what they have learned.

One of the most important results of the involved Sunday school class is what psychologists call ownership. When people make a personal investment in their learning, they own it and are responsible for it.

Thus, responsibility for success or failure is shared by each person rather than just the teacher. Such responsibility motivates people to work for success. In theological terms, that means people will own the responsibility of living out what they learn through involvement and self-discovery. The Bible refers to this as becoming "doers of the Word." This is a primary goal all church leaders should have. As a result of Sunday school, people should become responsible for expressing the church's mission by their actions.

As we approach the task of teaching believers of all ages about the church's mission, there is no better context than the Sunday school class.

It is possible for the pastor to deal with the church's mission from the pulpit, but the results in terms of learning will be slower than what can happen in Sunday school.

Hearing is a passive activity, allowing people to mentally disengage themselves from the learning process. Many people do not concentrate on the subject during a lecture. One homiletics professor reminded his students that while they are preaching, as many as 25 percent of their congregations may be daydreaming!

In contrast, a Sunday school class built upon the teaching principle of involvement learning tends to engage almost everyone throughout the session. (For a more detailed discussion of involvement learning, see *Learning Together* or *First Steps for Teachers,* available from Gospel Publishing House.)

People can learn more about the church's mission in a good Sunday school class than almost anywhere else. The sermon can then reinforce that learning and motivate believers to action.

A second advantage of the Sunday school class is the positive peer dynamic that can develop. Peer influence has a negative connotation in our society because of its definition in the teen culture. There we see peer influence pressuring teens into bad behavior and distorted values. Lost in that discussion is the truth that peer influence can be a positive force.

Positive peer influence is felt in a support group. Everyone needs a small group of people around him to empathize, encourage, guide, and provide accountability. When the peer group reflects godly values, Christian care, and body-life principles, it can be a force to mold strong, committed believers.

Such support groups take time to develop. They grow best in small-group settings. In the church, the largest small group ministry is the Sunday school. It must be mobilized as the central location for teaching the mission of the church and building support groups to motivate people to action.

Hindrances to the Sunday School's Effectiveness

Meaning and purpose in life are achieved through involvement in God's great mission. That mission should be learned and understood in Sunday school, but that does not always happen successfully. Why? Hindrances to the Sunday school's purpose do arise. We must remember we are engaged in a spiritual warfare. Satan, who is opposed to God's purpose, attempts to divert us from our mission. Let's examine several common hindrances that thwart the purpose of the Sunday school.

First, there's an artificial dichotomy between evangelism and education, resulting from an inadequate understanding of the Great Commission.

When I traveled to various churches as a seminar leader, I asked people to quote the Great Commission. The majority of the responses I received were in fact misquotes. They would say something like, "Go and make disciples," "Go into all the world and win the lost," or "Go and teach." These quotes reflect an inadequate understanding of our calling.

Let us examine what Jesus actually said. He defined a statement of mission with three components and then He provided a context.

1. *Make disciples.* Certainly this refers to the process of win-

ning people to Jesus Christ. But the object is to make *disciples.* That means something different from simply making believers who mentally assent to the system of God's truth. A true disciple is one who imitates his master. He is a doer whose desire is to love the Lord by obeying His commandments.

Our goal is to win people to Jesus who will become participators in mission.

During the late 1970s, George Gallup commissioned a poll in response to the nationwide attention being given to the idea of being born again. He wanted to find out how many born-again people there were in America. The results indicated the number to be in excess of 40 million.

If there were, in fact, more than 40 million true disciples of Jesus Christ in the United States, it would comprise one of the largest and most influential groups in the society. And, if they were working to obey Christ, many issues such as abortion, euthanasia, loss of personal freedoms, misuses of welfare systems, and so on would be corrected as Christians mobilized for service. But that is not happening. Why?

Could it be there are not really 40 million disciples of Jesus in this country? Is there instead a large group of people who believe in and acknowledge the idea of being born again, but they are not true disciples?

The mission Jesus gave us is to make disciples.

2. *Baptize converts.* After conversion, water baptism is the next logical step. It is the public act of affiliation and identification with the body of Christ.

What does that mean? We are never to lead people to Christ and then leave them alone. We have not fulfilled our mission until we help them become part of a local church. We are to accept responsibility for our new brothers and sisters in Christ. This has major implications for evangelism methods—Are they designed to incorporate people into the church or just to share a verbal message?

3. *Teach these new disciples to obey all that Christ commanded.* This is important for two reasons. Teaching equips the new disciple for service. He discovers what is expected of

Sunday School and Mission 27

Christians and he understands the mission to which he has been called. Further, he validates his love for Jesus by keeping His commandments.

Jesus placed this Great Commission in a powerful context. He said, "As you are going, I will be with you to the end."

Because Aramaic and Hebrew participles were sometimes used as imperatives, we have the translation, "Go ye." But the participial rendering would be "as you go." What a subtle, but powerful, difference! The imperative "go ye" implies we have the choice of going or not going. But the participial "as you go" implies that, in Jesus' mind, there was never a question that His followers would go. He simply assumed that if we were His disciples, we would be going. The imperative suggests we might decide to do something by participating in a program of witnessing or evangelism. The participial implies that whatever we do, wherever we go, we will be deeply motivated spiritually to share Christ as a natural reflection of our lives.

Furthermore, Jesus promised His constant and abiding presence to believers as they fulfill His mission. What wonderful news for the disciple!

Now, what does that mean to our discussion? People who see the Great Commission only in terms of going and making converts develop a misconception concerning the Christian education ministry of the church. Some suggest that evangelism is the very backbone of the church. They want to promote evangelism programs and training as the means for becoming a "real church."

The result is a very limited view of Christian education. Such churches often contact hundreds, but keep few of them. Or many people are won to the Lord, but never instructed. The church thus becomes immature, weak, and doctrinally confused.

The other extreme is to exalt Christian education as the focus of the church. Primary attention is given to nurturing those who already believe, creating a limited view of evangelism. The result will be churches that become introverted, lose their mission to serve those outside the church, and do not grow.

Inward and Outward Ministries

It is obvious that both extremes are wrong. There is no dichotomy of evangelism and Christian education. Evangelism and Christian education are inseparable. We will never train and motivate disciples to go into the world and make other disciples unless we inform them of their mission. We must teach converts to study to show themselves approved and to prepare to make a defense for the gospel.

On the other hand, our Christian education means little unless it is expressed in action, and the primary activity to which Jesus called us is winning people who do not know Him.

This is what George Peters, writing in *A Theology of Church Growth,* calls the inward and outward ministries. "The inward ministry of fellowship, education, edification, discipline, and structuring is designed to produce a responsible community. The outward ministry charts the relationship and responsibilities of the church to the world."[2]

These twins, evangelism and education, do not naturally occur in most churches. They must be cultivated. We must uncover the reality of evangelism and education for those who make up the church. That is a primary purpose of the Sunday school.

The Sunday school must be careful to define itself first in aggressive terms of mission rather than nurture. Yet, nurture must not be diminished. It is the means to the end, which is mission. We can fulfill our mission only as we realize that evangelism and Christian education are both components of Jesus' Great Commission to us.

Overemphasis on Worship Services

A second hindrance to the Sunday school's real purpose is the contemporary reaction against it. Sunday school has lost its excitement in some churches. Among mainline denominations the trend has been to eliminate Sunday school as a ministry arm of the church. Unfortunately we hear some of the same negativism expressed among evangelical and Pentecostal churches.

This is due in part to the bias of those who have been converted into our churches. Phenomenal growth occurred within the Assemblies of God during the 1970s and continued into this decade. Most of the people who presently attend Assemblies of God churches were not born or raised in these churches. We have been dramatically influenced by the charismatic renewal. Many charismatics settled into our churches, finding a church home there. However, from a religious-sociological perspective, charismatics—like Pentecostals at the turn of the century—are reactionary. That is to be expected. They are reacting against former church situations that were dry, uninteresting, and devoid of the joy and power of Christ at work. Many of them see Sunday school as part of their former, unfulfilling religious experience. Thus, it is not uncommon to find churches where worship attendance averages two or three times that of the Sunday school.

The error, of course, is blaming Sunday school for its lack of spirituality. In evangelical/Pentecostal churches, Sunday schools often are the most exciting and spiritually edifying places to be. Scores of people continue to be won to Christ through the Sunday school's ministry.

This trend to emphasize the worship services and deemphasize the Sunday school reflects an inadequate understanding of the church's twofold mission. People enjoy worship. That is perfectly proper because the first part of our mission is to worship and praise God. Yet, refusing to involve oneself in the discipling ministries of the church ignores the second part of our mission, to serve others. We learn how to express our service in the educational ministries because they provide a Christian laboratory setting in which we can begin to work out our faith.

One of the things that motivates us to worship God is hearing about His mighty acts in our past and present. These are things we learn in Sunday school. Thus, what happens in Sunday school motivates us to worship, making the Sunday school all the more important. Just as thinking of evangelism and education as two separate things is incorrect, so is the idea that worship and Sunday school are separate entities. If people are truly worshiping God, they will have a deep, intrinsic desire to be taught to fulfill their mission. Our love for Christ is expressed through obedience to His mission.

Another reason many churches react against Sunday school is that it has become little more than a dry, uninviting program. Some Sunday schools have little spiritual joy associated with them. They have been effectively "de-spiritualized" by organizational machinery. This is not to recommend a nonstructured approach. It is to warn of organizational traps hidden within organizational needs. When structure and organization become an end, the common perception will be that Sunday school is not spiritually edifying. When all our conversation about Sunday school deals with planning, training, promoting, and recruiting, we will inadvertently create an image of a program rather than a ministry. We need to replace the word *program* with *ministry.*

We can correct this problem by emphasizing the Sunday school's place in the church's mission, by highlighting the impact Sunday school is having on Christians, and by carefully defining it in terms of spiritual ministry.

Pastoral Leadership

Another hindrance to the Sunday school's fulfilling its purpose is the abdication of pastoral leadership. In far too many churches, pastors have delegated, and often relegated, leadership and influence in the Sunday school to others.

Certainly it is true that pastors cannot take direct leadership in every ministry, especially as churches grow. The problem described here occurs when pastors fail to see the importance of Sunday school and delegate it to others without any intent of personal involvement. These pastors know a Sunday school is needed, but they really do not want to be involved. Such an attitude almost always wounds the Sunday school ministry.

Most pastors probably get weary of hearing that they are the key to everything in the church. That can be overestimated. Nevertheless, it is true that the congregation looks to the pastor to determine what is happening in the church and the importance of various efforts.

In New Testament terms, the leader is one who goes ahead of the people and motions for them to catch up. He is to know the spiritual pulse of the church. He is seen as the primary administrator. He is perceived as a visionary. The goals, ministries, and organizations he implements have instant credibility.

It is, therefore, vital that the pastor have a strong commitment to Sunday school. He must personally involve himself in promoting it and educating the congregation about its purpose. Although the pastor need not personally direct the Sunday school, nothing can replace the value of his presence in a class, as a student or as the teacher. Some pastors resolutely refuse to teach because they believe it negatively affects their sermon presentation or is too time consuming. If that is the case, the pastor should be an example to his congregation by being part of a class. The congregation needs to know Sunday school has the full endorsement and commitment of the pastoral staff.

Furthermore, it is true that the pastor who teaches a class gains a forum for influencing his people that is not provided by other ministry outlets.

A primary purpose for the gift of pastor/teacher is to "prepare God's people for works of service" (Ephesians 4:12). However, it is often impossible for one person to accomplish that task; the wise pastor will look for support ministries to help him achieve this goal. The Sunday school is an effective ministry for helping him "equip the saints" (RSV).

Pastoral leadership and involvement are crucial to the success of the Sunday school.

Enculturation

A fourth hindrance to fulfilling the purpose of the Sunday

school is the enculturation of the church. Enculturation is the tendency of the church to reflect the secular culture around it. Enculturation is a spiritual issue and a subject of many Biblical warnings, yet it continues to be a problem.

Christians are called to be a unique and distinct people whose life-style, values, and relationships are very different from the secular world around them. Christians live in a special kingdom. They subscribe to a special ethical system. They approach life with a special intent and purpose.

When Christians begin to conform to secular values, ethics, and relationships, they deny their Christian identity. The Bible warns it is not possible to love God and the world at the same time, so we have to decide where our priorities lie.

When a society is knowledge-based, the priority is communication (speaking and hearing). The church is enculturated when this pursuit of knowledge alone is the priority. Certainly knowledge is important, but it is not the end; it is a means to an end. Sunday schools that emphasize only knowledge will never fulfill the second part of our mission: to serve others. When knowledge is the priority, then all that is necessary is to know about God, rather than to be acquainted with Him and serve Him. All that is required is to be a hearer of the Word. All that is expected of the Christian is to know Biblical content. It is obvious that this is inadequate, yet many Sunday schools function along these lines.

The Bible calls us to express what we know by what we do. The Bible teaches that we learn about God through what He did in history and what He continues to do in our lives. So the priority is not just communicating, but demonstrating. We love Christ by doing what He instructed. We are called to become doers of the Word.

The Sunday school that understands this will focus on helping people become doers. Those who teach and lead will never be satisfied just sharing information about God and the Bible. They will constantly strive for life application.

The Sunday school must be seen as a primary vehicle for accomplishing the church's mission. Those things that hinder the mission must be understood and corrected. Those who make up the church must commit themselves to involvement in the Sunday school.

NOTES

[1]Billie Davis, *Teaching To Meet Crisis Needs* (Springfield, MO: Gospel Publishing House, 1984), p. 7.

[2]George Peters, *A Theology of Church Growth* (Grand Rapids: Zondervan Publishing House, 1981), p. 185.

3
Laity and Mission

One analogy continually used to describe the church is that of an army. The militant church has come to signify the church aggressively and actively involved in its mission. It is reflected in many areas. Consider the phrases in our music: "A mighty fortress is our God, a bulwark never failing"; "Onward, Christian soldiers! marching as to war"; "O victory in Jesus, my Saviour, forever"; "Rise up, O men of God!" "A call for loyal soldiers comes to one and all; soldiers for the conflict, will you heed the call?" "We're marching to Zion."

In *Mere Christianity*, C. S. Lewis talks about the church's militancy. He suggests that Christians are like revolutionary soldiers whose mission is to win the world to Christ. These soldiers go to church to receive their marching orders so they will have clear direction to accomplish the task.

The militant church has always been and continues to be an apt description of what God's people should be. When people see themselves in militant terms, they are challenged to boldness and action. This is a particularly useful theme as we discuss laity and the mission of the church.

In his book *The Church Unleashed*, Frank Tillapaugh uses military terms to make a profound point. He writes that in wartime there are frontline and rear-echelon troops. He points out that these two groups of soldiers reflect two different attitudes. The frontline troops, those positioned directly in the battle, don't complain much. In the heat of the conflict they have little time for complaining. Because they are involved in the fighting, they quickly develop a camaraderie, a team spirit. They have to work together successfully to accomplish their strategy and win the battle. It is a matter of life and death. Such things as how the food tastes or where they will sleep matter little in light of the great issues that are being decided in battle.

The rear-echelon troops, those stationed a few miles behind the front lines of battle, are more apt to complain about circumstances—the food, weather, accommodations, officers. They are not part of the life and death struggle at the front. These men have difficulty seeing themselves involved in the struggle over great issues. They become preoccupied with the trivial. They do not need to be constantly on their guard. This attitude works against their effectiveness as fighting men.

The analogy has great application for the church in mission. Tillapaugh writes, "If we are involved in frontline ministries, we will be involved in people's lives. We will be dealing with them over issues such as salvation, repentance, spiritual growth, and deepening the level of fellowship with our Lord and other believers."[1]

When the laity find themselves in the real battle, they quickly develop good attitudes and a sense of team spirit. Battles are tough and sometimes painful, but Tillapaugh points out that being in the battle is much more meaningful than sitting around in the rear echelon.

While frontline soldiers of the Cross are wrestling with how they can win the world for Jesus Christ, those in the rear echelon tend to get bogged down in issues that waste time, talent, and treasures. We all know church members who argue over the color of carpets, or who will mow the grass, or what committees should be appointed next.

In the spiritual warfare the Bible describes, it is often enough of a victory for Satan if he can simply immobilize Christians. One of his chief goals is to get God's people off the front lines and back to the rear echelon where they will lose their sense of mission and aggressive spirit. Tillapaugh writes that a primary goal of frontline soldiers of the Cross is to see other people "rooted and built up in him [Christ], strengthened in the faith as you were taught, and overflowing with thankfulness" (Colossians 2:7). He affirms what good evangelicals have always known, that "frontline ministries happen through teaching or participation in a Sunday school class."[2]

The Aggressive Sunday School

No ministry is more equipped to recruit, train, equip, and mobilize the army of God than the Sunday school.

Consider the following results when the Sunday school focuses on the goal of mobilization:

1. *The Sunday school will define itself in aggressive, evangelistic terms.* We have previously stated that no dichotomy should occur between evangelism and education. They are two sides of a coin, and sequentially related: Christian education—nurture in the faith—leads to evangelism, and evangelism leads to nurture.

Sunday schools get into trouble when they lose sight of this truth. If the Sunday school exists only to nurture, it will be introverted. If it exists only to evangelize, it will be weak and immature. When education and evangelism are seen together, the Sunday school understands its mission is to win people who should then be discipled to win other people, and so on.

Because we understand that Jesus Christ is coming again, and billions still do not know Him, our mission becomes critical and must be defined in terms of aggressive, militant action. A Sunday school committed to moving its people to the front lines will be naturally, and visibly, evangelistic.

The Sunday school has always been a center for evangelistic efforts and it must continue to be so. Teachers and leaders must plan and serve with the focus of evangelism always in mind.

The overwhelming majority of people won to the church are reached through relationships with relatives, friends, neighbors, fellow employees, etc. Depending on the statistics used, it can be said that approximately 75 percent of those who affiliate with a church are won through such relationships. The small-group concept in Sunday school encourages members to invite their friends and associates to class. Many of those attracted will ultimately become part of the church.

Several years ago, my wife and I joined with another couple to begin an adult Sunday school class at our church. We began with four couples. It was our commitment from the beginning to emphasize relationships. We wanted to build a support group of caring individuals. We used teaching methods designed to promote our goals. In almost every class session we used small groups for discussions. Those groups not only increased the learning, but also built friendships. We encouraged sharing. We scheduled monthly socials.

The class grew. After 2 years, the class had an enrollment of 60 with an average attendance between 40 and 50. Those figures far exceeded what our facilities were capable of handling, but people were content to sit in crowded quarters because relationships had come to mean so much to them. And the class grew because members wanted their friends and relatives to share the experience.

That is how outreach and evangelism take place most effectively and naturally in Sunday school classes.

2. *The Sunday school will be a major vehicle for satisfying people's need for meaningful relationships.* The Bible calls Christians to a very intimate standard of relationships. If one person in the body of Christ hurts, others are supposed to empathize and respond. If one rejoices, everyone is supposed to share the celebration. Such relationships require openness and trust, two things that do not appear suddenly but have to be developed.

The church will not automatically manifest the quality of relationships to which the Bible calls it. So how can we achieve it? The church must develop ministries and opportunities for relationships to develop and grow. Any small-group ministry will help achieve this. The Sunday school is basically a small-group ministry, thus it becomes a primary center for relational development.

Our culture is so mechanized and technical that relationships are diminished in the pursuit of efficiency and production. People feel alienated from one another. They are treated as machines used to produce rather than as unique individuals with feelings. It is one of the sad ironies of our age that people can walk in a crowd and yet feel utterly alone.

In a world that tends toward dehumanization, the church must model exactly the opposite attitude. The church must resist enculturation. Those who serve as leaders must be vigilant and refuse to allow anything to take primary focus away from people. In the kingdom of God, people come first. Each individual is unique, important, and loved. That is part of the good news of the gospel. The church should be an oasis in a desert of loneliness. The very things people need and desire most—a little personal attention and love—can be provided by a good Sunday school class.

It is possible to do the Lord's work in the wrong way. It happens when we become so consumed with church business, programs, facilities, and plans that people are diminished. It happens when we've modeled the world's dehumanizing attitudes and our churches cease to meet people's needs for intimacy and relationships.

People who live and work in a dehumanizing world suffer identity crises. They lose their sense of worth and uniqueness. People need identity to help them feel secure and confident. In *Teaching To Meet Crisis Needs,* Billie Davis reminds us that "identity is a set of relationships and meanings. A person cannot find a ready-made identity, but must choose and develop his identity little by little from his life experiences."[3]

All individuals are made in God's image, objects of His love, and are valuable in His sight. The church must reflect that in every way possible.

3. *The Sunday school having an aggressive, militant goal will see people problems diminish.* People are unique and that uniqueness sometimes works to encourage dissension. In a congregation of 300 people, it is quite likely there will be 300 varying ideas of what the church should be, what the pastor should do, and how money should be spent. Left unattended, even an insignificant issue can explode in the congregation.

What can be done to prevent this? The question is important, for prevention is more valuable than corrective treatment.

The answer is to get as many people as possible into the frontline mission of the church. According to Larry Richards, noted Christian educator, the church's main objective should be getting lay people involved in ministry. He is right for two reasons.

First, when people become involved in frontline ministry, they are forced to focus their time, energy, and talents on the mission. They have little time left for gossip and quarreling. They begin to see their brothers and sisters as comrades in mission rather than adversaries with whom they must struggle. Diversity and differences fade when compared to the great mission we all share.

Second, involvement in frontline ministry creates an obedient church. Jesus measured love for himself in terms of obedience. When lay people are ministering, the church will be obeying the Great Commission, and God can express His purposes through the church.

People problems tend to have their source in an individual's own insecurity. A person who is dissatisfied with himself has difficulty ever being satisfied with others. When personal self-worth and meaning are missing, an individual is not emotionally, spiritually, or psychologically whole. As a result, he will not have healthy relationships.

Christ offers us abundant life, that is, life that is expressed in terms of wholeness, meaning, and well-being. But that quality of life is attained only through obedience and conformity to His purposes. When life is lived as Christ intends, it will reach its greatest expression. Such a life has worth, self-esteem, and significance. When people feel those things, they have little need to prove themselves to others. The need to dominate is eliminated. The need to control and manipulate is removed. Egos are brought under control and life can be enjoyed. Having learned to accept themselves, people are freed to accept others.

4. *An aggressive Sunday school tends to increase the desire for training among people.* The church is the largest volunteer

community in the world. Its existence depends on the giving of time, talents, and treasures to the kingdom of God as expressed through the local church. The church needs people to serve, but it needs people to serve well.

John Palmer reminded us in the 1986 training book that everyone is called to minister: "Participation [in ministry] is for everyone."[4] True, but there is a significant step between the moment a person discovers his gift of ministry and the time he bears fruit. That step is training.

Regardless of a person's gift, he or she will almost certainly need help and instruction to minister effectively. A person may be called to teach, but that alone does not make him a good teacher. His calling should motivate him toward training. Whether it be teaching, visiting, counseling, hospitality, or any service ministry, those who have been called need preparation. They need to learn people-helping skills, Biblical strategies, methods, and more.

What motivates people to seek such training? A desire to please God by serving effectively. If people sense the urgency of their task, if they understand that training makes them better Christian soldiers, if they want to do their best for God, then they will be willing to invest in training.

The Sunday school that focuses on mission and service will create a climate that inspires a desire for training.

Soldiers always undergo an initial, or basic, training. That is typically followed by a period in which they begin to function as soldiers while receiving specialized training. Then, they are assigned to a station of service to do that for which they have been prepared.

As militant Christians, we should do no less. Every Christian needs both basic and specialized training prior to being assigned. So the church should inspire a desire for training and also provide training opportunities.

5. *An aggressive Sunday school will help narrow the gap between the clergy and the laity.* Dr. Kenneth Van Wyk, writing about laity and clergy, pointed out the word *laity* comes from the Greek word *laikos.* "It designates those who belong

to the 'laos' or the chosen people of God. Thus, all who profess faith in Jesus Christ as Lord, men and women, are God's chosen 'laos.' "[5] Very simply, that means that everyone in the church belongs to one class of people. Clergy are part of the laity first.

The contemporary misunderstanding that professional clergy are assigned the task of Christian ministry thus freeing the laity from ministry responsibility is wrong. Yet it is expressed just that way in many churches.

Wherever the laity feel professional clergy are present to do all the ministry, the church will never be a dynamic, militant movement. God's call is to all men. The primary purpose of the clergy is to equip God's people to do the works of service to which God is calling them. Only in that way will the church be built up (Ephesians 4:11,12). The clergy are trainers, facilitators, and motivators.

Strategy for Training the Laity

Having identified several benefits that result when the Sunday school defines itself in aggressive terms, let us consider a strategy for educating and motivating the congregation.

1. *The church must explain its mission.* As in any army, the orders must be clear if they are to be followed. Leaders must enunciate the church's mission in terms that everyone can grasp. Often this is called stating a philosophy of ministry and it is very important. Developing a philosophy of ministry does several helpful things for a congregation.

   a. It clearly defines the purpose of the universal Church and how the local church will express it. Individual churches have different personalities. A philosophy tends to give a church identity.
   b. It establishes ministry goals that everyone can understand and work toward.
   c. It establishes priorities and identifies things that are not crucial to a local church.
   d. It pulls the entire congregation together around stated purposes so 100 people aren't going 100 directions.

A good Sunday school ought to have a well-defined philosophy of ministry. Several years ago, the national Sunday School Department provided a philosophy guideline called *Directions—The Way To Go for Sunday School Development.* When followed, *Directions* provides a philosophy that leads to quality Sunday schools.

Few people have done a better job of defining their mission than Ray Ortlund. In his book *Lord, Make My Life a Miracle* he tells how his church worked to develop a philosophy of ministry (sometimes called a statement of mission). Theirs was simple, yet profound and all-encompassing. It was stated in three priorities: Priority #1, "We are committed to God." Priority #2, "We are committed to the people of God." Priority #3, "We are committed to the work of God."

These statements were so clear and identifiable that everyone in the congregation knew them. They often identified various ministries according to their priority. Worship was a priority #1 ministry. The food bank was a priority #3 ministry.

The value of this idea lies in its clear enunciation to everyone of just what the mission is and its provision of an identifiable place for people to serve. Everyone knows what the church is about and what she is doing. When the orders are clear, the army follows effectively.

2. *The church must provide training for the laity.* When people volunteer to serve, they have a right to expect to be trained. Injustices are done to people when they volunteer to serve and are encouraged to do so without training or preparation. Untrained people usually fail. And, too often, leadership then considers them incapable. In truth, the real problem was taking a motivated, excited person and failing to give him what he needed to succeed.

People must be equipped for ministry. The Bible says so. Some of the training is directly from God through His Word and His Spirit. But much of it comes from His church.

Every church should have training programs. It is necessary to train enough people to adequately staff the vital ministries of the church. But it is equally necessary to have continual training courses from which to supply staff for growth, new ministries, and replacement.

Dr. Van Wyk offers four components for a workable lay training ministry. I will summarize them and add two of my own.

   a. Build momentum for lay involvement in the mission of the church. This can be done through a sermon series, a special Sunday school class, or an adult elective taught at some special time. The objective is to raise the level of understanding among the laity about ministry. This makes them accountable and builds motivation to serve.
   b. Develop a lay ministry identity. The pastor, acting with the Christian education program, must help the laity appreciate their importance in God's plan for the redemption of the world. Everyone has a personal part to play, and everyone must be led toward discovering what it is.
   c. Utilize Christ's pattern of discipling. His technique was to invest himself in a small group of people who could then invest themselves in a larger group, and so on. There is something powerful and permanent about pouring your life into someone else in a meaningful way.
   d. Develop a lay ministers training center. This could be a Bible study course, adult continuing class, or a variety of other options. It should include all of the above. It should include not only instruction but also opportunities to practice and experience what is being learned. It should be scheduled, having a starting and ending date. There is perhaps no greater format for this than a Sunday school class.[6]
   e. Make assignments. When people have completed their training and are aware of their mission and gifts, they need a specific assignment. There is something motivational about being asked to serve. Sit down with individuals and determine where they can best contribute to the mission of the church. Then give them the job.
   f. Follow-up. Although people recognize their gifts, understand their importance in the kingdom of God, obtain

training, and find a place to serve, they may still run into snags. They may experience insecurities or burnout. They may need a little moral support and encouragement. Therefore, it is imperative for leaders to follow up on their volunteers. Nothing replaces personal contact.

3. *The church must assign people effectively.* This is an elaboration of item "e" above. In an army the commander looks at all available personnel and deploys them in the most strategic manner for reaching his objectives. The same must be true of the church. Where do you need people? What kind of people do you need? Are they ready to serve?

Hundreds of people who would like to become involved in mission are simply sitting in the pew; they have not been recruited and deployed. We really do have an untapped army in our churches. Remember that our goal is to deploy people in frontline ministries where they will experience meaning and motivation. How can we do that?

First, we must do what Frank Tillapaugh suggests in *The Church Unleashed.* We must deliberately deemphasize the rear-echelon work in the church. Does it really matter who will repair the water cooler, or what brand of typing paper to purchase? It is counterproductive for these details to be major board decisions.

A common misconception holds that the presence of many committees means more meaningful lay involvement. The opposite is often true. Insignificant issues can get elevated to levels of exaggerated importance, while the real mission of the church goes unfulfilled. Let's involve everyone, but at the front lines of ministry.

We must learn to trust administrative matters to those who have been selected to make such decisions. If, as Larry Richards suggests, our greatest challenge is to get people involved in ministry, then we should ensure that our primary energy is devoted to that.

4. *The church must be constantly evaluating.* We are dealing with people, and that means changes all the time. Today we

may have a well-staffed Sunday school. Tomorrow, however, two families may be moving, two teachers want a sabbatical, one teacher may be pregnant, and another switch to Missionettes.

If we wait until such situations arise we will simply react, when we should act. We must be prepared for such eventualities. We can do that by evaluating. Certain evaluative questions should always be asked: How well are we doing now? What are our future needs? What can we do to improve ministry now? What resources do we need? How is our training effort progressing? Constantly asking such questions and responding to them ensures deliberate planning and acting rather than panicked reacting.

5. *The church must be prepared to make adjustments.* Very few things remain constant. Evaluation will do one of two things for us. It will confirm that we are doing well, or it will quickly identify areas where adjustments are needed. Both are desirable. If our ministries are not functioning well, they should be adjusted. Sometimes, midcourse corrections are necessary, imperative.

Good military leaders know when to withdraw, advance, turn the army to a flank position, or take the high ground. But such decisions are predicated on an evaluation of the circumstances, options, and effectiveness of the army in its present location.

Nothing kills ministry quicker than an inability to adapt. Whenever we deal with people we have no choice but to be flexible. We must avoid the fate of the church upon whose tombstone were inscribed these words, "We never did it that way before."

The church is meant to be an aggressive, militant army of believers. Everyone is important to the success of the mission to which Christ has called us. We must mobilize the lay army for the front lines.

NOTES

[1] Frank R. Tillapaugh, *The Church Unleashed* (Ventura, CA: Regal Books, 1978), p. 123.

[2]Ibid.

[3]Billie Davis, *Teaching To Meet Crisis Needs* (Springfield, MO: Gospel Publishing House, 1984), pp. 128-129.

[4]John Palmer, *Equipping for Ministry* (Springfield, MO: Gospel Publishing House, 1985), p. 27.

[5]Kenneth Van Wyk, "Training the Laity for Growing Churches," *Laity Training Resource Kit* (Garden Grove, CA: Garden Grove Community Church, 1975), p. 4.

[6]Ibid., pp. 7-9.

4
Preparing People for Mission

Let us begin this chapter by broadening the definition of *missionary*. Mention the word and most people immediately picture a man or woman, usually an ordained minister, wandering through the jungle telling the nationals about Christ. We often imagine missionaries wearing bush jackets and safari hats, riding in jeeps filled with supplies.

Missionaries are very different from what we often imagine. Today, entire families are stationed in countries throughout the world teaching, preaching, training, building, and evangelizing. Missionaries are all ages and appearances. They are as varied as people anywhere. They may be serving on a foreign field or in home missions. They may be serving 4-year tours or short-term assignments.

In all this variety we still tend to see them as people who specialize in reaching foreign, ethnic, or other unique groups around the world. We still think of them as someone different from us. That is the issue we must address.

In a strict sense, each of us is a missionary. We are people called to mission. We are involved in the twofold task of worshiping God and serving others. We are called to live out our mission of winning our neighbors, friends, relatives, and associates. We are missionaries to those around us. We are long-term in our communities. We've been given the assignment of saturating our neighborhoods with the gospel.

All committed members of the body of Christ must see themselves as missionaries. How we see ourselves tends to influence how we act. If we see ourselves as cowards, we will act shy and retiring. If we see ourselves as confident and capable, we will act outgoing and aggressive. If we see ourselves as great administrators, we will act that way. Similarly, if we see ourselves as missionaries, we will act in accordance with our perception.

It is a significant problem in the church that most people never see themselves as missionaries, and that diminishes their commitment to mission. We think of missionaries as people who have given God everything. They are sold out to their calling. We think that we can never attain that position. How tragic! Every one of us can be just that dedicated and committed to the cause of Christ.

So preparing people to actively take part in the mission of the church begins by teaching them that everyone who belongs to Christ is a missionary.

This is a challenge to the Sunday school and related Christian education ministries. We must evaluate and determine how effectively we are teaching this truth to every age-level. Every Christian must be accountable for how well he serves Christ. But accountability can result only when people understand to what they have been called.

Therefore, the Sunday school must teach believers what is expected of them. How can we do that? By teaching the following concepts:

1. *Every Christian is called to be a minister/missionary.* It is simply not Biblical to sit back and allow the professional clergy to do all the ministry. It is not obedient to ignore this truth that all are called. Jesus' invitation was to "whosoever will."

2. *Every Christian has been gifted to serve as a minister/missionary.* All are called, and all are gifted in some special area of service according to the will of God for their lives. It is incumbent upon each Christian to discover his gift. The church leadership should take an active part in helping people with that search.

3. *Every believer needs to be trained for ministry.* A strong theology of training is apparent throughout the Bible. God

expects our best. We are to strive for excellence and effectiveness. God has provided leaders in the church to assist us as we learn to minister well. Every called and gifted person should have a desire for training.

4. *Every believer is important and interdependent with others in the body of Christ.* The church functions best in concert rather than in solos. What one person does in ministry is integrally related to what others do. Each person plays a part that relates to others and their areas of calling and giftedness. The analogy of all believers to Christ's body is a testimony to the mutual relationships and dependence that are necessary for the church to accomplish its mission.

5. *Every believer can help accomplish the church's mission.* How often we hear Christians engaged in self-depreciation, saying, "Yes, I know God calls everybody, but I'm just so incapable," or, "I have nothing to offer." Sometimes that is a genuine feeling, but often it is a way of rationalizing avoidance of responsibility and the hard work that comes with mission. Either way, it is wrong. When God calls people, He also equips them. He never makes mistakes. The Holy Spirit provides power and wisdom to accomplish whatever task lies before us.

6. *Every believer is accountable to God for the service rendered.* Few transgressions in an army are worse than disobedience and being AWOL (absent without leave). An army of disobedient soldiers will never win a battle. It takes a disciplined, obedient army to respond quickly and aggressively. Because generals have information the common foot soldier lacks, they often issue commands that seem to defy explanation to the soldier in the field. Yet, the general knows his orders are right—and he knows why he issues them. The soldier must trust his general enough to accept the order and accomplish it without hesitation. The same is true of Christian soldiers. God knows things we don't. It is imperative that we trust Him and obey, even when we don't understand. Only in that way can the mission be accomplished.

Obedience is one of the lost words of contemporary Christianity. We need to regain it. Jesus taught that if we really love Him, we will obey His words. We will be accountable to God for the quality of our obedience.

Being absent without leave is a terrible transgression. Soldiers are counted on to be ready to serve at a moment's notice. They are to be vigilant. It they need a rest, they receive leave, which ensures that the army knows where they are in case they are needed. To be absent without leave means the soldier cannot be depended on.

Christians sometimes act like they are AWOL. They refuse to serve, hide in the pews, and cannot be depended on to accomplish the church's mission. It is a terrible hindrance to the church when people go AWOL.

We are expected to produce—bear fruit. It we do not, we will ultimately be accountable to God.

The Sunday school can teach these truths at every age-level, and it should. Children can learn early that they are called and gifted. They can be trained to serve while they are young and impressionable, understanding that they are important in the plan of God.

We must be careful to set these truths in a proper context. Many people have a distorted, negative view of God that has developed from a poor self-concept, improper teaching, or a legalistic concept of Christianity. Regardless of the reason, if people view God as stern, demanding, and judgmental, they will hear these truths as "demandments," uttered to oppress us and induce more guilt.

We must carefully teach that God loves us and that we are created in His image with incredible potential and worth. Because He loves us so, He has chosen to partner with us to accomplish His great purpose for mankind. We are in a noble and privileged position as His children. The idea of being called and gifted, trained and placed in relationship with others, is great news. It should never be cause for fear or guilt.

We must teach our children that the greatest joy in life results from being part of God's plan.

When Christians understand what is expected of them, they

should be motivated to respond positively. At that point, we can help teach people to become missionaries.

Being a Missionary Starts in the Heart

Human beings have a tendency to want the sweet corn without working in the garden. We want the glamorous things without having to experience the mundane. We want the thrill of victory without the hard work of preparation.

Being an avid baseball fan, I have watched the careers of many young men who had great natural ability to run, hit, and field on a baseball diamond. Yet many of them lasted only a few seasons. On the other hand, some men who lacked great natural ability have played professionally for 15-plus seasons with great success.

What makes the difference? Natural ability alone is not enough to guarantee success. Great baseball players learn and practice the fundamentals of the game. They have incredible desire that drives them to play with excellence. The difference between the gifted player who is short-term and the average player who has a long career is in the heart. The one who is committed and loves the game deeply excels.

Becoming a missionary on God's team starts in the heart. If the desire to please God is strong, then the person will commit himself to the task, whatever it takes.

Learning the fundamentals is as important to the Christian as it is to the athlete. What are the fundamentals for believers? They are found in Galatians 5:22,23. We call them the fruit of the Spirit: love, joy, peace, patience, kindness, goodness, faithfulness, gentleness, and self-control. Why are these fundamentals for Christians?

The answer lies in the truth that good ministry flows out of good character.

The Holy Spirit provides two great things for us, fruit and gifts. Fruit relates to our character, what kind of people we are on the inside. Gifts relate to our ministry, what we do. Gifts are occasional in our lives. We exercise them as opportunities for ministry arise. Fruit is constant in our lives and should be manifested in all we do. Fruit is important because it establishes the context and foundation of our ministry.

Fruit	Gifts
of the	of the
Spirit	Spirit

Character ———→ leads to ———→ Ministry

We all know sad stories of people who have attempted to minister out of bad character. They may appear to be successful and people may be unaware of their character problems. But, eventually, something happens and their bad character is exposed. The result? Credibility is ruined, the Christian ministry is discredited, and leadership is placed under suspicion. Ministry must begin in the heart.

The implications of this truth are important to the Sunday school. The Sunday school is a primary center for people-helping, according to Billie Davis. I have proposed that it is a primary center for teaching the mission of the church. It is also a center for teaching Christian life-style. The Sunday school class is often the first place in the church where we are taught to love, be joyful, patient, kind, and faithful. These fundamental Christian traits are taught and modeled for us; early in life we learn what a missionary's character is like.

Apart from parents, perhaps no other person exerts a more powerful influence in helping the student understand the meaning of being a Christian than a Sunday school teacher. The teacher models Christlikeness for the students. As he ministers to the students, he demonstrates character. When the teacher's character is right (he loves the students, is patient, kind, etc.), his ministry is received. When his character is out of line, his ministry is often rejected.

When a teacher instructs the class that gossip is a sin, and then is overheard in the hall gossiping about a fellow Christian, the positive influence of the lesson is lost in the negative example and *hypocrisy* is modeled instead.

Sunday school should be a place where Christian character is taught and expressed through the teacher. It is the Sunday school teacher who guides individuals to prepare for Christian mission by helping mold their hearts.

Sunday School and Faith-Shaping

All new Christians go through a process of faith-shaping. As new believers our faith is exciting, but embryonic. We have new life, but ahead of us we have much to learn. As we grow in Christ, we experience great joys, but also some tough moments as we learn that being a Christian means sacrifice and sometimes suffering. Our faith goes through a reshaping process as it grows and matures.

It is important that the church be a safe environment in which faith-shaping can occur. Consider an example.

Most teenagers, at some point, wrestle with the existence of God. Even teens who have been raised in the church may struggle with this issue. Because they question the existence of God does not mean they are atheists. Rather, it probably means they are grappling with the implications of God's presence. The reality of God is an abstract and deep thing to consider, even for adults.

Suppose a teen named John came to his Sunday school teacher one day and said, "Mr. Jones, I've been doing a lot of thinking lately, and I'm not sure there is a God."

Mr. Jones has two options. His first is to call the pastor and deacons, force John to his knees, and pray for conviction to descend. Doing that will probably convince John that God either is not real or is abusive.

Mr. Jones' second option is to ask John to sit down, lovingly look him straight in the eye, and share a personal experience from his own life when he wrestled with the same issue.

If Mr. Jones takes the second approach, he will convey several powerful truths to John, by both word and action.

1. John will know he is accepted and loved regardless of his questions.

2. John will know he is not weird or sinful for expressing the truth of his struggle.

3. John will know it is okay and safe to share honest feelings in church.

4. John will see an example of someone who wrestled with the same issue and overcame it.

Using the second option will teach John a powerful lesson about the love and acceptance of Jesus Christ. It will help him relax and know he is acceptable, even when he is struggling. Such an experience will become an important building block in John's faith-shaping. He will probably refer back to the experience as a time when Christ touched his life through a Sunday school teacher. Such experiences both teach and model proper Christian character, which is a prerequisite for Christian ministry.

The Sunday school class should be a place where faith-development and maturing can take place in a safe, accepting, and encouraging atmosphere. Such an atmosphere builds and edifies people. It puts them on the road to becoming strong missionaries.

What Does a Disciple Called to Mission Look Like?

Thus far, we have said that the Sunday school must help believers understand what is expected of them. It must help believers prepare their hearts, for ministry flows from the heart. The Sunday school must provide an atmosphere where faith can be questioned, shaped, and matured without condemnation or rejection.

Now, let us consider the distinguishing traits apparent in the lives of mature missionaries.

1. *A missionary-disciple is identified by love.* Jesus set the standard in John 13:34,35. We are to love one another as Christ loved us, that is, by laying down our lives for one another. It

will be that quality of love that convinces men we are truly Christians.

2. *A missionary-disciple is willing to serve.* Again, it was Jesus who set the standard in Mark 10:45. Jesus came to serve by giving up His life. Further, He told His disciples after the footwashing in John 13 that they would be blessed only as they served one another. Serving is the second part of the twofold mission of the church. When we are truly imitators of the Master, we will be eager to serve others.

3. *A missionary-disciple is teachable.* He listens, learns, and changes. Disciples are not stubborn or set in their ways. In St. Joseph, Missouri, where the wagon trains began the trek westward, may be seen an old, authentic sign that instructed the wagon drivers, "Pick your rut carefully. You will be in it all the way to California." Some Christians ride their entire lives in the same old ruts. They are not teachable. A teachable disciple can accept the instruction that will strengthen his life, even if that instruction hurts.

4. *A missionary-disciple is submissive to authority.* He recognizes that he must be submissive both to God and to those whom God has established as leaders in the church. A submissive disciple responds even when he does not completely understand or even enjoy what he is being asked to do. This disciple does not demand his own way.

5. *A missionary-disciple is forgiving.* A person who knows how to forgive will usually express good relationships in every other area. This disciple realizes that he has been forgiven. He is in touch with his own weaknesses and knows that he is not perfect. He understands that forgiveness flows to him all the time. As a grateful recipient of God's forgiveness, he freely forgives others.

6. *A missionary-disciple has integrity.* Integrity means he will stand for what is right. His motives are pure and honest. Because he has integrity he will be courageous, standing alone if necessary rather than compromising his character or faith. Such disciples know life holds truth that is worth dying for.

7. *A missionary-disciple is not concerned with material pos-*

sessions. One of the most tragic figures in the New Testament is a young man named Demas. At one time Demas had a dynamic ministry. He was so successful that he was allowed to minister with Paul. However, in the last mention of this young man in the Scriptures, Paul writes that Demas had forsaken him because he loved the world more than he loved God.

We are warned in the Scriptures that we cannot serve two masters. We cannot love the world and love God at the same time. Making concerns about material things a priority dilutes our devotion to Christ, and we cease being His true disciples.

8. *A missionary-disciple is obedient and faithful.* His desire is to please God in every way. He can be counted on and trusted.

9. *A missionary-disciple knows what his mission is.* He has clear direction. He does not wander aimlessly through life. His priorities are in order.

10. *A missionary-disciple enjoys life.* Life is a celebration. He knows what abundant life means. He has joy and confidence that show. He knows how to laugh and rejoice. He can live life victoriously because the joy of the Lord has become his strength.

In the Sunday school our goal should be to produce people who can be described by these traits. As we teach Biblical information, it is equally important to teach believers to model happy hearts and good character.

It is not without significance that some people who can't read and write still manifest the most Christlike character. Ironically, some people know the Bible and can quote many verses, but their attitudes are sinful, and they do not even profess faith in Christ.

Sunday school should make people thoroughly Christian, rather than simply fill their minds with information.

Throughout the New Testament, people are called to become "perfect." That word does not mean "without flaw." Rather, in Greek, it refers to something becoming what it was created and intended to be. A glass that is filled with a liquid of some sort has become perfect. It is being used as it was created and intended.

For the Christian, becoming perfect means being what God

created us to be. It involves maturity that is demonstrated in proper relationships, character, and attitudes. This sort of maturity makes us valuable to God and useful in accomplishing His mission for mankind.

This maturity qualifies people for leadership. It is not surprising that in his book *The Measure of a Man* Gene Getz uses the Biblical description for leaders as a guideline for maturity in men. It is logical. Our goal is to grow up in Christ, to be conformed to His image. When that happens, we are qualified for leadership in the kingdom of God, either by appointment or example.

Those who become the greatest missionaries have grown into maturity. They have become what God created them to be.

We must ask ourselves these important questions: "Is our Sunday school helping to produce people like those described above? If not, what can we do to change our Sunday school so it will reach this goal?"

James Smart addresses the issue in thought-provoking fashion. He cites the failure of individual Christians to function as missionaries when he writes,

> The missionary situation of the Church in the twentieth century calls for a Church in which each member, as he comes up against the unbelieving world, will be able to bear effective witness to his faith, both in word and action.... In humiliation, we must confess that we are not ready for the missionary situation that is upon us. The word "missions" denotes an activity sponsored by us in non-Christian lands, or in distant parts of our lands, or in underprivileged sections of our city, and not the occupation of ordinary church members. Our churches "have" missions, but they are not themselves ... missionaries....[1]

Kenneth Van Wyk writes that the "need of the church is to devise an educational program geared to equip believers to invade the world of unbelief and bear witness to the Truth of the Christian faith. In other words, Christian education needs to be task-oriented."[2]

Our task is to build strong disciples who see themselves as

missionaries whose priority is to participate in the mission of the church. The Sunday school faces few challenges any greater than this.

NOTES

[1] James D. Smart, *The Teaching Ministry of the Church* (Philadelphia: Westminster Press, 1954), pp. 99-100.

[2] Kenneth Van Wyk, "The Purpose of Christian Education," *Laity Training Resource Kit* (Garden Grove, CA: Garden Grove Community Church, 1975), p. 4.

5
Witness and Mission

One of the greatest expenditures of business money each year in America is for advertising. Billions of dollars are spent to promote, persuade, and sell. In the automobile industry alone, multiplied millions of dollars are spent to attract people into the showroom—largely on the basis of image. We can hardly imagine the investment in advertising made by tobacco and alcohol-related industries. It is staggering to realize that so much money, effort, and time are devoted to persuading the public to buy. The effort is so great that advertising itself is an enormous industry.

What makes all this persuasion successful? Several theories—positive and negative—are put forward. Some advertising is built upon simply *creating* a need for a product. If people are told in many ways, and often, that they need something, soon they will believe it. That is a very manipulative form of persuasion, yet people respond to it.

Opposite this approach is advertising that responds to legitimate human needs. Knowing a need exists, the advertising simply presents options and products.

Subliminal advertising represents another negative extreme. Subtle and persuasive messages are disguised in visual and sound media like films and music. Though the messages are detected only at the subconscious level, they are nevertheless effective. This extremely negative and manipulative advertising is illegal in some areas.

This discussion reminds us that at the heart of persuasion should lie confidence and integrity. People can be persuaded about ideas and products honestly or dishonestly. They can be manipulated or left to make independent decisions based on evaluation and reason.

Some very interesting studies have been conducted related to politicians and their ability to persuade voters. Apparently, in the average voter's mind, the issues at stake in most elections take a backseat to how the character of the politician is perceived. If the individual is perceived as honest, the voter is willing to trust him even if they do not always agree on issues. On the other hand, a candidate perceived as dishonest is never trusted, even if he takes the same position as the voter. However, people can be very fickle about what determines their perceptions of honesty or dishonesty.

As Christians, we are involved in persuading people to consider and receive Jesus Christ. Witness and evangelism are a primary part of our mission as the church. And they involve what we say, how we act, what we are like on the inside, and how we are perceived by those to whom we witness.

The Christian who genuinely desires to please God by effectively fulfilling his mission will take great care how he shares his faith. If our mission is to make disciples, then how we do that is crucial.

The New Testament clearly emphasizes the importance of *every* Christian being a witness; it is a means God has established for winning the world to Christ. Dr. James Kennedy (founder of Evangelism Explosion) illustrates that point.

> If a gifted evangelist with an international reputation could win 1,000 persons for Christ every night of the year, it would take him over 10,000 years to win the whole world to Christ. But if one true disciple of Christ were able under God to win just one person each year and train that person to win one other person each year, it would take only 32 years to win the whole world for Christ![1]

Kennedy further states that churches that take seriously the need to train Christians for evangelism rarely need special evangelistic services, yet they consistently win many people to Christ.

What does this mean? We must realize that taking the mission of the church seriously requires us to train every Christian to be a witness and participate in the evangelization of the world.

What Is the Problem?

It is a non sequitur to think in terms of a silent Christian. For a Christian, telling others about Jesus Christ should be as natural as breathing, eating, or sleeping.

The Bible seems to say that we become overcomers based on two things: the work of Jesus Christ on our behalf ("the blood of the Lamb") and our willingness to tell others about it ("the word of their testimony"—Revelation 12:11). So sharing Christ is valuable to our successfully living the Christian life. However, Jesus' call to us was not entirely for our own benefit. His church has been called out for the sake of others. Jesus was our example in this. He did not come to be served, but to serve and give up His life for others (Mark 10:45).

We are given the mission of telling others about Jesus. The Bible teaches that as we do we gain strength and become overcomers. Yet, we sadly acknowledge that most Christians simply do not share Christ very effectively. Several evangelical churches, in an attempt to evaluate the success of their evangelism efforts, have conducted surveys and found startling results. Apparently most evangelical believers win only a few people to Christ in their lifetimes. Some never do.

What is wrong? How can such an important part of our mission be so neglected? We are forced to consider possible answers to those questions.

1. Perhaps Christians do not believe what we teach and preach about the value of evangelism. It has been written that we act on those things that are truly of value to us. If witnessing for Christ were really important to us, we would respond by actively sharing Christ.

At the core of this problem is the issue of commitment to God's Word. It is apparent in the Scriptures that winning the people of the world to Christ is God's primary purpose. It is not God's will that any person should perish. We are to go into the world and make disciples. God's method is to work through His people.

The Bible is clear. To doubt such an obvious teaching is to neglect the authority of God's Word.

2. Perhaps Christians doubt the work of the Holy Spirit. Certainly many believers neglect their witness because of fear, lack of confidence, and timidity. Yet Jesus taught that His Spirit would be sent to empower and enable us for our mission of evangelizing the world. The Holy Spirit's work includes helping us deal with our self-doubts and hesitation. We must, however, *allow* Him to help us.

3. Perhaps some Christians are selfish and unconcerned about the more than 2 billion people who have never heard the gospel. If that is true, the attitude itself betrays a lack of sanctification and love. It is possible for believers to be self-centered, but that is not what Christ desires. At the very center of Christianity lies the servant's heart that propels one to serve others. Jesus died for even those who would not receive Him. How can we not be willing to follow His example?

4. Perhaps some Christians are lazy. We are not talking about the sort of laziness that causes people to sit and do nothing. Most Christians are very busy. But there is a laziness that keeps believers from doing the *right* things. We all tend to busy our lives with scores of things that will ultimately mean little or nothing in eternity. It takes effort and energy to change the priorities in our lives and commit ourselves to things that truly matter.

5. Probably the real reason most believers neglect witness and evangelism is because they have not been adequately challenged and trained to accomplish their part of the church's mission.

People need to be trained to witness effectively. This is incumbent in the Great Commission where Jesus instructs the disciples to teach new converts "to obey everything I have commanded" (Matthew 28:20).

If the Church is to evangelize the entire world, then each Christian must be trained to fulfill his part of the mission. Though it may be natural to share Christ with some people, it is necessary to be trained in order to share Him with others. If serious questions about Christianity arise, the believer is admonished to be prepared to make a defense for the gospel (1 Peter 3:15). Defending the gospel is something we must learn to do. It is predicated on a solid understanding of the Scriptures, Christian doctrine, and theology.

Training is necessary to help us understand evangelism methods. We might need to share Christ with a Moslem in a different way than we might share with an agnostic. Such distinctions can be learned to increase the effectiveness of our witness.

Training is also necessary to build commitment to mission. As evangelical-Pentecostal believers, we commit ourselves to what we know to be Biblical. It is important to teach every believer that sharing Christ is a Biblical expectation. One reason the majority of Christians do not successfully share Christ with others may be the lack of commitment to that part of their mission.

Recently, I went to Honduras with a team of 20 other people to build a church. For several days as we labored on the construction we noticed two handsome young Mormon missionaries who walked the dusty, hot roads of the village to tell the Hondurans about Mormonism. Though we disagreed with their doctrine and theology, we admired their commitment to tell other people about it.

It is a common occurrence to turn on our televisions and hear the evening news describe revolutionaries who fight to the point of death for their causes. If we could harness that sort of commitment and apply it to the cause of Christ, we might, in fact, realize the goal of winning the world. We must begin with teaching our people to be accountable to God's Word and the mission as described there.

To return to our original illustration, if business is willing to spend billions of dollars persuading masses of people to purchase unnecessary goods, to what extent should we be willing to prepare to win those same masses to Christ?

Preparing People for Evangelism

The question we must now consider is how do we prepare believers to accept their evangelistic mission?

First, we should define terms. Peter Wagner has pointed out that being a witness for Christ and being an evangelist for Christ are two different things. Everyone is called to be a witness for Christ but not all are called to serve as evangelists. All Christians must be committed to the church's mission of evangelism, but not all are gifted as evangelists. Though only a minority of church members may be gifted in evangelism, that does not relieve the responsibility we all have to be witnesses. We must perform our part of the mission of the church to win the world to Christ.

It is not logical to argue that because one is not gifted as an evangelist, he is freed from the task of sharing Christ. That would be a contradiction of the New Testament's intent.

Knowing, then, that all believers are to be witnesses, we must define the word. A witness has five identifying traits:

1. *A witness must have firsthand experience.* Of what are we witnesses? What is the substance, or content, we want to share? Our witness has to be what Jesus has done in our own lives. Testifying to the life-changing power of God if it had not personally happened to us would be ridiculous and counterproductive.

One of the reasons the Early Church grew so rapidly was the truth behind the descriptive words. They could easily tell people about Jesus Christ and His resurrection because they had seen and experienced the events of which they spoke. Furthermore, those with whom they shared would also have known that their words were true.

The best witness is the one with an authentic experience.

2. *A witness must be able to adequately express himself.* Communication is a learned skill. Thus, training believers to

communicate the gospel is imperative. The whole concept of friendship evangelism is based on teaching believers how best to communicate Christ to their family and friends. Effective Christian witnessing is an ability that can be developed.

3. *A witness should be motivated by compassion for those who do not know Christ.* Jesus was moved with compassion for people. He loved and cared for them all. We must constantly remind ourselves that all men are made in God's image and, therefore, have worth and importance. God desires that they all be restored to Him.

4. *A witness should be obedient.* Genuine Christianity is reflected in a desire to please God. Jesus said our love for Him would be measured by the degree of our obedience to His words. A witness will share Christ because he loves his Lord.

5. *A witness knows the Holy Spirit will use his efforts to accomplish God's purposes.* We must always remember it is our responsibility to share the good news of Christ. We do not save anyone. That is God's work as His Spirit draws people to Christ. A witness shares, knowing the Holy Spirit can use simple words and deeds to accomplish great things. A witness will faithfully tell others about Jesus, trusting the Holy Spirit to touch hearts and break down barriers to the gospel. Such confidence in the Spirit's work makes a witness strong and courageous. A witness does not predetermine the outcome. He simply tells about Jesus.

Sharing the Message

Having defined what it means to be a witness, let us examine the content of our message. What does a witness tell? Once again, certain components cannot be left out of the content we share if our message is to be complete.

1. *What we say must be Christ-centered.* The Book of Acts repeatedly describes how the early disciples proclaimed the centrality of Jesus Christ. The entire revelation of God to mankind centers on Jesus Christ. He is like no one else. He is the reason for a Christian's being. He has given us a story to tell. Without Him, we have nothing to say. Thus, when we share,

we center on Christ. In some way, we must tell His story: His life, teaching, death, and resurrection.

2. *We must share the conditions of the gospel.* What are the implications of the Incarnation? Why did Christ come? What did His death and resurrection mean? The gospel makes it plain that Christ came to reconcile man to God (see 2 Corinthians 5:18). The gospel means sharing the love of God and how to receive it (i.e., how to be saved).

These elements of being Christ-centered and sharing the conditions of the gospel must be verbalized, but they must also be reflected in our lives (see 2 Corinthians 5:20). God makes His appeal through us. What we say about Christ will be validated or invalidated by what is apparent in our own lives. Persuading people requires that they can clearly see in our life-styles what they hear us say with our mouths.

Furthermore, sharing the gospel must be complete. We are not permitted to neglect any part of it. Though it is "good news" it also includes carrying the cross of the suffering Servant. We are to tell the entire truth to those with whom we share. We are not to preach what Dietrich Bonhoeffer called cheap grace. Commitment has a price and it must be boldly shared.

3. *We should emphasize God's power.* The gospel is appealing because it offers hope of reconciliation to God and recovery of life. Because God is powerful and at work in human affairs, we know wounded, ruined lives can be restored. The gospel of Jesus Christ offers hope.

Early in this chapter we considered negative and positive theories of advertising. Persuasion that is manipulative or dishonest is never right, even though it may produce apparently good results. Right and wrong cannot be determined by sales statistics.

The same principle holds true for Christian evangelism. We are not to manipulate or coerce people. Because we know all men are created in God's image, we work to preserve the integrity and worth of every individual. We do not treat people as objects to be controlled or statistics to be counted. We are to value each individual and share Christ with him in a loving, caring way. If people feel they are being manipulated or pressured, they will reject both the witness and his message.

As we witness, we should use wisdom to do so in the most productive way possible. This includes being sensitive to what David Watson calls "the right man, the right time, the right words."[2]

1. *The right man* means that "we observe what the Spirit is doing in people's lives, and, boldly and sensitively, take the opportunities God sends."[3] God prepares people and situations. We should be watching for them.

2. *The right time* means God works with time in the process of evangelism. We might witness to a man at a point in his life when his heart is cold and rejecting. Two years later, he may receive the gospel message and turn to Christ. God prepares people and situations in His time. We should learn to be sensitive to them.

3. *The right words* means being sensitive to say things that are relevant to the person to whom we are witnessing. Are we listening to the Spirit speak to our hearts the right words to say? Are we selecting words and ideas with which the recipient can identify? Are our words simple enough to be clearly understood?

Preparing People Through the Sunday School

We have pointed out previously that the Sunday school was born in evangelism and it continues to be a primary source for the evangelistic ministries of the church.

With that in mind and considering the content of this chapter, we must consider how the Sunday school can practically assist believers in preparing for their evangelism mission.

1. *The Sunday school should provide a consistent and continuing emphasis on evangelism.* The Sunday school must remember its roots and avoid the temptation to be only a nurturing ministry. We are preparing people for a purpose (i.e., to glorify God and win the world for His kingdom). Every teacher and leader must share the commitment to make evangelism a

priority. Evangelism should be mentioned often and encouraged in a variety of ways throughout the Sunday school. The entire staff should have a clear, working knowledge of evangelism and its components.

2. *The Sunday school should provide thorough Biblical training in evangelism.* Our people have a high sense of accountability to the Bible. That being true, the Sunday school must explain exactly what the Bible has to say and how we can become "doers of the Word" in evangelism. This training should start early, in the elementary classes, and never stop. If we teach our children how to be successful witnesses for Christ, we will not have to reteach them as teens and adults.

3. *The Sunday school should give people opportunities to practice.* In the sciences, few things contribute more to learning than the laboratory. There, students can practice and do things to confirm what they are learning.

Few people are naturally endowed to be successful witnesses. It is helpful to learn skills to assist us as we share the gospel. The Sunday school should provide the lab experience. This can be done by means of roleplays, simulation games, or actual witnessing experiences that are evaluated and discussed in class.

Another means by which this lab experience can be provided is by designing classes expressly for the purpose of evangelism training. A Life-Style Evangelism class and an Evangelism Explosion class are examples. Often the Sunday school hour is the best time of the week to provide such training.

4. *The Sunday school should provide a forum in which believers can share the result of their witnessing efforts.* Frequently, we do not realize what wonderful things God is doing around us because we have no place where people can share.

In classes where evangelism is being emphasized, time should be given to share both successes and failures. Successes provide a cause for rejoicing; failures provide a motivation for prayer. Sharing also helps build a support group of people with similar experiences who can encourage and support one another. Sharing builds community and body-life. It creates the feeling that everyone "owns" the efforts of each individual. That is what Paul was teaching in 1 Corinthians 12. When we allow people to share about their efforts, everyone identifies, prays, rejoices, encourages, edifies, and is motivated to become involved themselves.

5. *Perhaps one of the most important things the Sunday school can do is provide leaders and teachers who are effective models.* It will never be enough to have a teacher who simply talks about evangelism. Teachers must understand their mission and speak from practical experience as well as objective Biblical truth.

As the people of God we are called to persuade others to consider the truth about Jesus. We have that right, given to us by our Lord. We are called to do it well as one of our priority functions. We will never fulfill our mission as the Church without learning the basic truth, that we are called to help win the world for Christ.

NOTES

[1] David Watson, *Called and Committed* (Wheaton, IL: Harold Shaw Publishers, 1982), p. 45.
[2] Ibid, pp. 151,152.
[3] Ibid, p. 152.

6

Doctrine and Mission

Doctrine. Say the word three times. How does it make you feel? Few people would say that repeating the word *doctrine* makes them feel excited, motivated, and warm all over.

Perhaps we do not have to feel like we are on an emotional high when thinking about doctrine. After all, theological studies of any kind require hard thinking and commitment. On the other hand, far too many Pentecostal/charismatic believers have a destructive prejudice against the very mention of the word *doctrine.*

It is not unusual to hear comments like, "We need men who will preach the Word instead of doctrine." Or, "Let's talk about the joy of the Lord and His benefits rather than doctrine." Or, "Doctrine is bondage, but the Spirit gives liberty." The implication is that any pastor or teacher who chooses to teach doctrinal studies is placing people in bondage and quenching the work of the Holy Spirit. That very attitude exposes the lack of sound doctrinal instruction.

The prejudice against doctrine comes from two strong sources, one traditional, the other, modern. Some classical Pentecostals have had a long-standing prejudice against education. When the classical Pentecostal denominations were born early in this century, they were reacting against religious systems that had gone to extremes in education, even to the point of denying the authority and accuracy of the Bible. Such extremes influenced the mainline churches, robbing them of their evangelistic zeal and emphasis on personal piety. The result was churches out of Biblical balance, emphasizing a social gospel rather than redemption through the work of Jesus Christ.

More and more people in mainline churches rejected what was happening in the training of their clergy and began to seek God. At the same time, Pentecostal groups emerged as God poured out His Spirit on those seeking Him. Many of the men and women attracted to these new movements were good and simple people. Yet some of them brought to their new churches a prejudice against education born out of their own lack of formal training.

That, coupled with the educational extremes of the mainline churches, gave the new Pentecostal groups a reactionary, antieducational bent.

As our churches have matured and begun to understand the strong theology of Biblical education, the prejudices have diminished. But among us remains some prejudice against formal ministerial training, especially seminary training. Consequently, our denomination still struggles to adequately fund our Bible colleges and seminary. There is still some reaction against exegetical preaching and a preference for lecture-type teaching rather than the more educationally sound, involvement learning methods.

A contemporary source reflecting a disdain for doctrine has come from the charismatic renewal. Though recent, it parallels the reactionary response of traditional Pentecostals 80 years ago.

Most charismatic believers have come from churches in which they felt unfulfilled and cold. Many of their former churches were strong in doctrinal-theological studies, but lacking in the genuine life and movement of the Holy Spirit. Through the renewal, many of their people found church homes that were exciting and spiritually alive. Their response was to reject everything associated with their church past and embrace the new. So anything that reminded them of the past—Sunday school, doctrine, exegetical preaching—was considered worldly or the traditions of men.

Thus, a sermon series dealing with what we believe, a Sunday school class about doctrine and theology, may create little interest. (Note: Though the modern prejudice against doctrinal studies is still strong, it is diminishing. This has been in reaction, in no small part, to the abundance of teaching in the electronic media, much of which is contradictory or extreme. Like the Early Church, which canonized the Bible in response to heretical teachings, the Pentecostal/charismatic church is now being forced to reconsider sound doctrine and theology as a way of dealing with extremes and heresies.)

Nevertheless, despite some believers' prejudice toward doctrine, they do accept doctrine. Regardless of a person's emotional reactions, doctrine of one kind or another still forms the basis of what he believes. He may deny the importance of doctrine, but he still embraces it. And though he might ridicule theological studies, he has a theology to which he is strongly attached.

A dichotomy between doctrine and "freedom in the Spirit" is artificial, unbiblical, and unhealthy for believers. The life and freedom we have in the Spirit is available to us only because we understand the Biblical doctrine of the Holy Spirit.

The theme of this book is the mission of the church. So the question before us is what is the relationship between mission and doctrine?

The great missionary-teacher Henrick Kraemer has written that all lay activity we plan will "ultimately fail if it has no lasting and serious theological foundation."[1] Kenneth Van Wyk wrote, "The proper starting point . . . is not program ideas but rather the Biblical foundation undergirding the program."[2] That can be said for any activity of the church, but especially its mission.

The Importance of Doctrine

Though we call it doctrine, theology, or simply knowing what we believe, each of us must have a clear understanding of what it means to be a Christian and what our mission is in order to live successfully as God intends. Let us consider why doctrine is so important.

1. *Doctrine is necessary to our Christian witness.* Peter tells

us in the New Testament to be prepared to make a defense for the hope that is within us (1 Peter 3:15). We should be able to articulate what we believe about our hope and why we believe it. That requires having doctrinal information. If we say we believe Jesus Christ has saved us from our sins, we need to explain how and why. If we say we believe He is coming again, we need to be able to support that from God's Word.

It is a sad reality that those who belong to cults and other religions often do a far better job explaining what they believe and why than do born-again Christians.

Paul told Timothy he should study to be approved as a young Christian leader. What does approval mean? In Paul's context, it meant to become a teacher who knew how to handle God's Word correctly (2 Timothy 2:15).

We live in an age when everyone seems to have opinions about the Scriptures. Often these views are contradictory, purely subjective, existential, or even heretical. We must have a standard of objective truth by which we measure opinions, ideas, and philosophies. Sound doctrine, as it is contained in the objective Word of God, is our standard. Thus, we can affirm what our Statement of Fundamental Truths says, "The Bible is our all sufficient rule for faith and practice, . . . the authoritative rule of faith and conduct."

Another irony of our day is that evangelicals, who profess a life or death commitment to the inerrant Word of God, often are most guilty of holding subjective opinions about it. God's Word cannot mean 100 different things to 100 different people. We must find out what it meant when it was inspired and written and what that truth means to us today. This pursuit results in a solid Biblical doctrine we should embrace and be able to explain.

Being a faithful, effective witness means to tell the story of what Jesus Christ has done. It also means being able and willing to explain and defend the validity of the gospel.

2. *Sound doctrine is necessary to being the church.* In our culture, there are many concepts of what a church is. From the Bible, we know a real church does four things: worship, disciple,

witness, and fellowship. It is impossible to have an effective discipleship ministry that does not include study and training in doctrine.

Notice the Early Church's example. Immediately after the outpouring of the Holy Spirit, as thousands received Jesus Christ, believers started coming together as the church. What sorts of things did they do? Acts 2:42–47 describes it beautifully. They had fellowship because they had discovered a new commonality in Christ that bound them together. They prayed together. They shared meals. In fact, their value system changed so radically that they shared all things. Signs and miracles took place among them. They became regular attenders at the temple. They praised and worshiped God and their numbers grew dramatically.

Having said all that, let us now go back to Acts 2:42 and notice the first thing they did. They devoted themselves to the study of the apostles' doctrine and teaching! The Holy Spirit began to help them understand the Scriptures. They began to truly understand who Jesus was and why He had come, and it changed every area of their lives.

To be the church means to devote ourselves to the study and acceptance of doctrine.

3. *Doctrine is necessary for maintaining balance in our lives.* Being Pentecostal in doctrine and practice means certain things. For one, it means we emphasize experience and encourage an experiential walk with Christ. That position contains some risk, for it allows a great deal of subjectivity, but we believe God speaks to the daily affairs of men.

At the same time, we also believe God never changes and that Jesus Christ is the same yesterday, today, and forever. Thus, God will never move or speak apart from, or in contradiction to, what we know about Him in the objective Word of God.

People can gravitate to either extreme. At one end are those who are not open to the possibility that the Holy Spirit can quicken our hearts and minds, giving us direction and guidance for our own unique circumstances and situations today. At the opposite end are those who believe what they feel in their hearts and minds is more authoritative than the Word of God.

God expects us to maintain a balance between the Word and our experience. If all we have is experience, our lives are in danger of becoming totally existential. We are built on a subjective base that will wash away when the storms come. But if all we have is an academic approach to Bible study, our faith may become dry and unexciting, devoid of the joy flowing out of abundant life.

We need balance. Our experiences with the living Lord give vitality to our understanding of His Word. But it is our commitment to the objective Word of God—with all its doctrine and theology—that keeps our subjective experience from leading us into existentialism and extreme or false teaching. Our experience must always be measured and validated by what God's Word teaches.

A proper understanding of sound doctrine is used by God to help us maintain the sort of dynamic balance Pentecostal believers enjoy.

4. *Doctrine provides an identity.* What is the difference between a Buddhist, Hindu, or Moslem, and a Christian? What is the difference between a Methodist and a Presbyterian, an Episcopalian and a Catholic? What is the difference between a Baptist or Nazarene and an Assemblies of God member? In some cases the difference is in organizational structure and polity (that is, church government). But between denominations a significant difference in doctrine as well as polity almost always exists.

We are uniquely Assemblies of God people because we believe certain theological doctrines. That does not mean we are extremely different from our brother evangelicals/Pentecostals. In fact, most evangelicals agree on five fundamental points of doctrine (the Virgin Birth, the resurrection and deity of Christ, His substitutionary atonement, the Second Coming, and the authority and inerrancy of the Bible). What makes us unique is our distinctive mix of doctrine, polity, and tradition.

Identity is important in life. Knowing who we are gives us a place to stand. It provides security and self-assurance.

In *Teaching To Meet Crisis Needs,* Billie Davis points out that "identity as a Christian involves making a decision about a personal relationship with Christ. . . . The search for identity is a search for somebody and something to identify with, to make a commitment to."[3] That decision for Christ and the subsequent commitments to His body and teachings have a doctrinal basis. Our spiritual identity is tied to doctrine. In simple terms, we know who we are because we know what the Bible says about us and what we believe.

5. *Doctrine guides us to the truth.* We live in a society that resists commitment to objective, ultimate truth. The prevailing philosophy in the secular world is, Let everyone have his own private notion of truth. Instead of identifying right and wrong, the world takes the attitude that what's right for you may be wrong for me and vice versa. Everything is subjective and relative.

When someone comes along and says that ultimate, objective truth does exist and man should commit himself to it, the secular world is convicted of its ambivalence and relativity. So the secular world protests and calls those who define the truth narrow-minded or ignorant.

We must say here that there *is* truth to which we can commit ourselves. In this world are good and evil, and it is important to know the difference. The basis for successful living now and eternal life later is built on our commitment to truth. We born-again Christians believe this so strongly that we are engaged in the evangelistic effort to tell the entire world about it.

Because objective truth does exist, that which is not true also exists. *Theology* means "the study of God." It is entirely possible for people to study God and never know Him. It is also possible to study God and come to wrong conclusions about Him. In other words, people can embrace false theology and doctrine. It is imperative that people learn to differentiate between sound doctrine and false doctrine.

Some would suggest we can avoid this problem by eliminating doctrine altogether. "Just pray, go to church, and enjoy your experience with the Spirit" may sound like good advice, but it isn't. Many sincere believers pray, go to church, enjoy their faith, and still find it difficult to differentiate between true and false teaching.

The best solution is the hardest: We must study doctrine and discover the truth. God has established the church as the context in which that pursuit should take place. The church provides the setting through which God reveals His truth. As believers study God's Word in the context of the body of Christ, the Holy Spirit will guide them into the truth. That is a doctrinal pursuit.

The explosion of technology has resulted in a proliferation of media ministries. We are all thankful that the gospel can be spread around the world by means of television and radio. But anyone can use the media—even those who have no doctrinal base, a false doctrinal base, poor character, or simply an inability to rightly divide God's Word.

The result is chaotic, because anything that comes across the media automatically has an air of authority; Marshall McLuhan was correct when he said that the medium itself is the message. Doctrinal study makes God's Word absolutely central. God intends for the location of doctrinal study of His Word to be in the church, where it can be both taught and lived out with accountability and integrity. There, the truth can be learned and lived. This is not to indict all media ministries not directly connected to the church, but to stress that such ministries should be accountable and submissive to the church as they engage in teaching the Bible.

6. *Doctrine is the roadmap of our mission.* Our doctrine of salvation defines our mission in evangelism. Our doctrine of God and the Church defines our mission in worship. Our doctrine of the body of Christ defines our mission in fellowship. Our doctrine of God's Word defines our mission in discipleship and Christian education. Knowing sound doctrine outlines how we should live and what our purpose is. Neglecting doctrine may doom us to failure in our mission.

Sunday School as a Primary Center for Doctrinal Study

For some years a battle has raged over which is most important: *knowing, being,* or *doing.* Whenever the discussion is heard, *knowing* always appears to lose. Usually the debate goes something like this: Who you are is more important than what you know or what you do. Or, what you do is more important than what you know because doing proves what you are (being).

Perhaps such observations are correct, but making these distinctions among the three seems to come down to simply an intellectual exercise, having no practical purpose. The truth is they are not either/or propositions. They are connected, interrelated. One flows out of the other.

The kind of persons we become and the way in which we live are profoundly influenced by what we know to be right and proper. We become accountable to what we know and bring our lives into conformity to that which we recognize to be true.

When it comes to being a Christian "doer of the Word," we discover what that means as we learn what the Bible teaches. That requires knowing something.

Knowing is never enough by itself, but it is absolutely foundational to the being and doing that follow. That has great implications for Sunday schools. From time to time the Sunday school wrestles to rediscover its purpose. At times it has been defined as an evangelistic ministry, at other times as a fellowship ministry. Occasionally it has been seen as a place to mold Christian lives or as a center of church growth.

Sunday schools are all those things and more, but let us never forget that a central purpose of the Sunday school is to teach students to know the Bible. We should never deemphasize the content purpose of Sunday school. If we are not teaching our students to know God's Word, then we will raise a church that is Biblically illiterate and subject to any false or shallow teaching that presents itself.

How well we teach the Bible, its theology and doctrine, determines the strength of our church. Teaching people to know the Bible counters heretical drifts and fosters security among believers as they learn to embrace together God's whole truth.

The Sunday school ministry will always be multifaceted, but one of its primary goals must be teaching believers to know the Bible well.

What are some specific things Sunday schools should do to ensure the teaching of sound doctrine, which will also ensure that our mission is being explained accurately to our people?

1. *Those responsible for the Sunday school must do all they can to guarantee the doctrinal position of their staff.* Nothing is more destructive than a Sunday school teacher who incorrectly handles the Word, especially a teacher who instructs children and new believers. When teachers are recruited they should be interviewed about doctrine. We should never permit individuals who embrace bad doctrine or theology to teach.

Teachers are powerful people in their influence; children believe whatever the teacher says. A child or new believer who does not have the maturity or Biblical knowledge to analyze what is taught may accept bad teaching as if it were true because it comes from a significant authority figure.

James 3:1 places the burden of integrity in teaching on the teacher. We will be especially accountable for the content and manner of our teaching. That should give a would-be teacher pause, for no one should teach without also accepting the responsibility that accompanies the calling.

No one is infallible, but we can be sure that we teach sound doctrine by (1) being a student of doctrinal and theological study, (2) learning to clearly articulate what we believe, (3) regularly teaching the Statement of Fundamental Truths, and (4) following the curriculum prepared for us. Prepared curriculum has been edited to ensure proper doctrinal and theological content. A major problem of allowing a teacher to teach whatever he wants is that it removes the careful and accurate doctrinal presentation provided by a good printed curriculum.

David Watson, in his book *Called and Committed,* says that some unbiblical movements arise because of a lack of doctrinal and moral discipline. We need to enforce a commitment to right theology. He writes,

> When ordained clergymen openly deny Christ's divinity or reject His bodily resurrection or permit sexual immorality, clear discipline is needed. Given the need for compassion when any Christian, including a leader, is wrestling with honest doubts, we need also the courage to stop such a theology or teacher from exercising a public ministry while working through his other personal uncertainties.[4]

Pastors, superintendents, and Christian education committees must ensure that teachers instruct in sound doctrine. Ultimately, that will be more important than the curriculum, facilities, follow-up, enlargement campaign, and so on.

2. *The Sunday school should provide classes designed especially for instruction in doctrine.* This usually takes the form of a new believers or converts class. That is acceptable yet it misses a significant group, namely, those who have been in the church for some time but have never studied what they believe and why they believe it.

Identifying new believers is easy. Identifying those who gradually come into the church, often from other churches, is more difficult. Usually already having accepted Christ, they move into the life of the church with an appearance of being well-grounded in the faith. Because they have a church background, it is often assumed they need no doctrinal instruction. Yet, these good people, who come to Assemblies of God churches because they love what they find there, can be totally ignorant of what it means to be an evangelical/Pentecostal believer. We should make an effort to place all our new people—whether converts or transfers from other churches—in a doctrine class.

3. *We should teach so that the student can articulate what he believes.* It is not enough to have the teacher explain doctrine. The students must have opportunity to state it in their own words in an accurate and convincing manner. Our goal is to disciple believers who can make a defense for the hope that

is within them. Sunday school classes must provide the laboratory experience for learning to express doctrinal belief.

A recent survey finds a greater interest in adult education than ever before in our history. More adults are enrolled in some form of continuing education than the total number of children enrolled in elementary and high schools in the country. Adults are more educated than ever before. The literacy rate in the United States is one of the highest in the world. People are subjected to a constant stream of information, explanation, commentary, and thought-provocation.

When we approach the average nonbeliever about the gospel, he likely will raise many questions and some arguments that seem quite logical to him. We cannot allow ourselves to be intimidated by questions or intellectual resistance. We are to stand firm and know how to articulate the gospel, explaining why we accept it and even defending it when necessary.

People will not accept that which they perceive to be intellectually dishonest. Though accepting Christ may be ultimately a matter of the will, a convinced mind becomes a powerful determinant in swaying the will.

The Sunday school is the place where we can instruct our people in doctrine most quickly and effectively.

In light of what we have discussed in this chapter, say the word *doctrine* three times. How does it feel now? It is sound doctrine that helps us understand our mission and makes us accountable for being spiritually intelligent "doers of the Word."

NOTES

[1]Henrick Kraemer, *A Theology of the Laity* (Philadelphia: Westminster Press, 1958), p. 13.

[2]Kenneth Van Wyk, "Training the Laity for Growing Churches," *Laity Training Resource Kit* (Garden Grove, CA: Garden Grove Community Church, 1975), p. 3.

[3]Billie Davis, *Teaching To Meet Crisis Needs* (Springfield, MO: Gospel Publishing House, 1984), p. 130.

[4]David Watson, *Called and Committed* (Wheaton, IL: Harold Shaw Publishers, 1982), p. 43.

7
Worship and Mission

What's a chapter about worship doing in a Christian education training book? We are studying the church's mission and it is our position, as previously stated, that worship is a priority of that mission.

As a matter of fact, the important link between Christian education and worship is too often neglected.

The intent here, however, is not to outline a theology of worship. That has been done skillfully by a variety of writers. Rather, we will consider three things: (1) a brief, general discussion of worship, (2) an examination of the relationship between worship and Christian education, especially as it is expressed through the Sunday school, and (3) a consideration of the Sunday school as a center for teaching about worship.

The Priority of Worship

A. W. Tozer once wrote that worship is "the missing jewel of the church." His description of worship as a jewel is appropriate. Of all the things a church does, none is more precious and beautiful than worship.

The people of God have been called a "chosen race, a royal priesthood, a holy nation, God's own people, that [they] may declare the wonderful deeds of him who called [them] out of darkness into his marvelous light" (1 Peter 2:9, RSV).

This chosen race and royal priesthood has been given the assignment to "declare his glory among the nations." They are to "ascribe to the Lord glory and strength" and "the glory due his name" (1 Chronicles 16:24,28,29).

Furthermore, the Bible teaches that as believers make worshiping God a priority, good works flow out of their lives. Jesus said, "Let your light shine before men in such a way that they may see your good works, and glorify your Father who is in heaven" (Matthew 5:16, NASB). The implication is that the good works that flow out of us will lead others to worship God.

Worship is innate. All human beings are created to worship. Not all worship God, but everyone worships something.

What is worship? A strict definition would include attributing worth to God. Many ideas about what is and is not worship are current today. Usually, these ideas stem from personal preferences for certain worship forms and expressions. Some people think good worship is loud, large, and loose. That means lots of noise, large crowds, and little or no order. Some think good worship is silent, small, and staid. That means it is quiet, formal, and best experienced in small groups. Some people think we have not truly worshiped without an hour of praise choruses. Others think we have not worshiped unless the pastor has sermonized for an hour.

Who's right? In a sense, everyone is. Within the Biblical principles governing worship (see 1 Corinthians 12 to 14), a great variety of expression is allowed.

Worship tends to be influenced by both culture and personality. I have visited churches in Latin America. In some of those churches the worship is noisy and busy and often takes place every night of the year. It is much different from our worship in the United States.

Is Latin American worship better than ours? No. Is our worship better than Latin America's? Certainly not. The worship is different because each culture has its worship forms and people have differing preferences in their expressions.

Some people, when worshiping, love to lift their hands and shout praises to God. Others prefer to bow their heads and weep. Is one expression better than the other? No.

Such varieties of expression are a testimony to the great freedom Pentecostal/charismatic worshipers possess. God looks at the content of the heart. Then He allows us tremendous freedom in expressing what is within us. Acceptable worship is founded on spirit and truth (see John 4:23,24).

Someone once wrote that every act of man can be an act of worship if man so desires. How true! We can attribute worth to God in all we do if we set our minds to it (see Colossians 3:17).

We must remember that worship is something we do to express what is inside us. Robert E. Webber, professor of theology at Wheaton College, wrote a book titled *Worship Is a Verb*. What a fitting definition!

The philosopher/theologian Soren Kierkegaard said that in worship, God is the audience, the congregation are the performers, and the worship leaders are the prompters. What we do in worship is for God, who is watching.

We have a tendency to confuse the roles. We sometimes act as if the leaders are the performers, God is the prompter, and the congregation is the audience. That is not worship.

Webber says that "worship is a verb. It is not something done to us or for us, but by us."[1] Pentecostal theology has always acknowledged and allowed for that. Long ago, we took seriously the teaching of 1 Corinthians 14:26-33. Everyone has something to give and do in worship.

Our worship services must allow for every believer to participate in a significant way. We must have times when people can do things together to worship and adore God. Yet we are not to be just loud, large, and loose. Our worship is governed by the standard of God's Word even as it is inspired and motivated by God's Spirit.

We seek the dynamic balance between the Word and the Spirit, mentioned in an earlier chapter. David Watson summarized the extremes and the balance in *I Believe in Evangelism:*

> "All Word and no Spirit—we dry up;
> All Spirit and no Word—we blow up;
> Word and Spirit—we grow up."[2]

Worship includes many components, which should all be brought into play: praise, thanksgiving, offerings, meditation, reading and hearing the Word of God, the Lord's Supper, prayer, and gifts of the Spirit.

Each is important to God, and He desires that they all be manifested as His people worship. But human beings have a tendency to be faddish. They also have a propensity for extremes. I can recall when the major emphasis of worship was prayer. No service was complete, or even acceptable, unless believers spent half an hour to an hour praying at the altars at the conclusion of every service.

Then came a time when preaching was central. It seemed as if we rushed through all the other components of worship to get to the sermon, which was given 45 minutes or an hour. Presently, there is a great emphasis on praise.

Perhaps the Lord sends these emphases to correct areas of omission, but we are not to vacillate to extremes, choosing one component over all the others. God wants us to do all the things mentioned, and do them to His glory. Both privately and corporately, we are to praise Him. We are to thank Him and pray and give our tithes and offerings. We are to gather around His Word and celebrate His presence in Communion. We are to manifest the gifts of the Spirit. All is to be done to His glory. These are things we do for Him.

Most of all, worship cannot be selfish or it becomes idolatry. This is a difficult problem. It is easy to slip into a mentality that says, "I worship to get something." The church has been tainted by the narcissism of the 1970s with its emphasis on "me."

In *Furnace of Renewal*, George Mallone wrote,

> In many churches, this egocentricity has been baptized in the name of worship. We are now coaxed to church with phrases like "Come, you'll feel better," "Worship and you'll prosper," "Praise and you'll be healed." Christians should not be bribed to worship. A parent will often resort to bribery to get a child to finish a meal. "You'll get some nice cake if you finish your carrots." That may work for a

while, but sooner or later it will fail. Without internal motivation there can be no genuine response. Likewise in worship, believers must be moved internally by the majesty of God's presence.[3]

We do not worship to get anything. We do not worship to have an experience. We worship for one reason only, because God is God and He is worthy of our adoration. Anything less is manipulative and selfish and cancels real worship by substituting a humanism disguised in religious trappings.

Mallone cautions that selfishness can be masked by innocent statements like, "Did you enjoy the worship service today?" He terms this the "filling station" view of worship, in which the worshiper comes to be refueled with all he needs to make it through another week. He continues,

> Whether we enjoy it or not, are comfortable or not, none of these areas is a sufficient criterion for measuring worship. Rather, the test of any worship should be, "What did God receive from it? What did I put into it? Did God enjoy the worship? Was He pleased by the sacrifice of our praise and our service? Or was He discontent because our wills, emotions, and intellect were disengaged in the process?"[4]

We can worship God sacrificially and unselfishly even when we don't feel like it or simply don't want to. Why? Because worship is something we do based on the objective truth about God. It is not predicated on our feelings.

When I recognize that worship is for God, that it is something I do to adore Him, and that I have incredible freedom of expression, my relationship with Him comes alive in a marvelous expression of joy.

Discovering and "polishing" the "missing jewel of the church" is one of the most important things a believer will ever accomplish.

The Link Between Christian Education and Worship

Though we have an innate desire to worship, and though the

Holy Spirit may prompt us to respond to God, much of what we know about worship is learned in the community of faith we call the church. Our zeal to worship is based on knowledge, and that is where Christian education is vitally linked with worship.

Christian education may not be worship for most people, but it is certainly the pursuit in which we learn much about worship. I saw this vividly in the church where my family and I attended several years ago. One Sunday morning I looked up at the balcony where I saw about 30 children and four teachers. The students were about 8 years old. During the worship service they watched, asked questions, and gathered around one of the teachers for some sort of discussion or explanation. I was so intrigued that after the service I asked about what I had seen. I discovered that our Sunday school ministry included a class for 8-year-olds designed to teach them about worship and prepare them to participate in it. When those children would join their families in congregational worship at age 9 (which was also part of the design), they would have a good understanding of what was taking place, and why, as well as how they could respond as worshipers themselves.

Of all the things Sunday school classes could have provided those children, few would mean more to the long-term development of Christian practice than this preparation-for-worship class. And, it is important to note, it was a Christian education ministry taking place in Sunday school.

Sunday school can be a primary center for teaching about worship. However, it should not be in competition with the worship service.

Recently I had a conversation with a gentleman about a Sunday school class he enjoyed greatly. I asked why it was such a good experience for him. He explained that he loved the class because people sang and prayed together. Often, he reported, the gifts of the Spirit were manifested and extended times of prayer for people's needs would occur.

We should never prohibit manifestations like those described above in Sunday school. However, what was occurring was a worship service. The people in the class were participating in a "pre-service" rather than a Sunday school class. Had the content of the class been a study of worship, such active participation and practice might have been very appropriate. However, the subject matter of the class was an Old Testament book study.

Worship and Sunday school have distinct identities. Attempting to make a worship service out of a Sunday school class creates an imbalance between zeal and knowledge, favoring zeal.

The Sunday school must recognize and assume its identity: It is a place to teach and learn. Worship ought to be one of its topics, but Sunday school itself should not be in competition with the worship service. Rather, Sunday school can complement worship. In Sunday school I can learn what worship is, why I do it, and how. In the service, I have a chance to experience and put into practice what I have learned.

This means the Sunday school must both teach and encourage worship. It is not enough for believers to know about worship; they must become doers of worship as well.

Sunday school classes, especially at the youth and adult levels, must teach how the priesthood of believers relates to worship. We believe that as a priesthood of believers, all men and women can approach God. Robert Webber says this principle encourages everyone to become involved in offering the worship of praise and thanksgiving to the Father.[5]

Because we are a priesthood of believers, we must all worship. We are not to accept the idea of worship as entertainment of the congregation or as the domain of a few (that is, those on the platform).

The priesthood of all believers concept also means the entire congregation worships together as the body of Christ. Sunday school can create in people an accountability by explaining what the Bible teaches and what God expects of each believer.

Though the Sunday school is a center of teaching about worship, we must ensure that we do not go to educational extremes. We are not simply to teach about worship and act as if that is our primary objective. The ultimate goal of Christian education is to change people, helping them conform to the image of Christ. We want to help believers become authentic worshipers.

To accomplish that we may not need to teach people so much about worship as about God. As we teach them about God—His attributes, plan for redemption, and promises for the future—people will naturally be drawn toward worship.

The fact is that as Sunday schools do a good job of teaching the Bible, a natural by-product should be better worship. In this simple equation lies the vital link between Christian education and worship.

The Sunday School as a Teaching Center for Worship

We've said several times that Sunday school classes should be used to teach believers to be better worshipers. But how do we teach for "doing"? Simply giving information is inadequate. We have to teach using a strategy that invokes an active response. Let us consider several things the Sunday school can teach to increase both involvement in, and the quality of, worship.

1. *The Sunday school can be an agent of change.* Learning can be defined as change. Worship sometimes grows boring and lifeless because of people's unwillingness to change. However, our people have a high regard for that which they believe to be Biblical. Thus, the Sunday school by teaching the Bible will help broaden the boundaries of worship. We should challenge people to open up to new expressions of worship. We should teach them to rediscover the vitality of worship. The teaching function of the Sunday school can help people increase their vision for worship. Learning is change and the Sunday school can be a powerful agent of change in the church. This is especially true for enlarging the understanding of worship.

2. *The Sunday school can teach the profound truth that worship happens best in community with fellow believers.* Although it is important to be a private worshiper, we are all created to worship together. Worship is not to be seen as oc-

curring in isolation. It is a contradiction in terms to think of people coming to church and having a private worship experience apart from their brothers and sisters. My worship is best when I am thinking of my brothers and sisters. That is why Paul spends so much time in Corinthians establishing the corporate context for worship. Worship is like a body with all parts functioning in concert (1 Corinthians 12). Worship is useless unless it is built on love for others (1 Corinthians 13). Worship means I yield my own agenda, my own list of expectations, giving preference to my brothers and sisters, and follow rules for worship, knowing this will allow everyone to participate as God intends (1 Corinthians 14).

We must teach our people to cultivate a corporate vision for worship. As the Sunday school fulfills its fellowship function, the idea of corporate worship will probably occur naturally. Why? When people care deeply about one another, it spills over into all areas of life. Real fellowship builds caring relationships.

3. *The Sunday school should teach that real worship is never selfish.* We are not really receiving in worship as much as we should be giving to God. It is a dangerous thing to encourage a congregation to approach worship to receive what God has for them, for such language creates the impression that we are there to get rather than to give. God may do special things for people during worship, but it will be because of His grace, not because of a cause and effect relationship.

Responding to the question, "Why are so many people bored in our Sunday morning worship services?" Pastor Robert Schmidgall said,

> Specifically, we're going to the worship service with a list of spoken and unspoken requests. We're not entering into fellowship as 1 Corinthians 14 teaches—to bring a hymn, a word of instruction, an uplifting thought that will help the entire body. We all bring our hidden agendas, and when our personal agendas are not the center of focus, we're disappointed and then bored.[6]

Such an attitude results from a selfish orientation toward

worship. One of the greatest services the Sunday school can render is to begin teaching as early as possible that worship is something I do for God more than for myself. If we train our children correctly, we will raise good worshipers who will have an unselfish attitude as they approach God.

4. *Sunday school teachers must understand worship.* Once again, we must focus on the teachers. It is imperative that teachers have a proper understanding of worship, for what they teach and model will speak louder than any curriculum they use.

Ask yourself, Do I as a teacher talk about worship in terms of what one can get from it? Or do I describe worship in terms of offering praise and adoration to God? Am I a positive role model in the worship services? Do I have a clear Biblical definition of worship? What is the leadership of the Sunday school doing to ensure that the teaching staff offers positive instruction about worship?

5. *The Sunday school must give some primary attention to teaching about worship symbols.* It is shocking to discover how little our people understand the meaningfulness of our worship symbols, such as the bread and juice of Communion.

Because we are nonliturgical and Pentecostal, we find the thought of worship symbols alien. We feel that way not because we do not have symbols. Rather, it is because we do not understand what they are and how they influence us.

Robert Webber recalls a conversation with David Mains about symbols in worship. He quotes Mains as saying,

> If Christ came physically, and actually stood in the midst of a people at worship, worship would begin with a symbol, not words. We would probably kneel, maybe even fall prostrate before Him.
>
> We would be so overwhelmed by God's presence that we would be at a loss for words. Kneeling or lying prostrate before Him would say it all. It's an action worth a thousand words. In His great wisdom and deep caring, God has given us some primary symbols in worship which are worth a thousand words.[7]

Are we teaching our students what Communion really means so they are adequately prepared to participate? When our students see the Bible at the front of the church do they immediately appreciate what it means? Do they think of its divine inspiration and protection in transmission? Do they think of it as their standard of faith and practice? Most of all, are we instructing our students to participate in the symbols and appreciate the depth of their significance?

6. *The Sunday school should stress preparation for worship.* In a very general way, we must teach our people to take worship more seriously. In far too many cases, people come into the sanctuary, engage in a little warm-up period, and then individually attempt to worship, having little concern for their brothers and sisters. Such an approach is shallow and introverted.

True worship requires preparation. Robert Schmidgall, in the article mentioned previously, recalled his childhood Saturday night ritual of the entire family doing things in preparation for church on Sunday morning. As he looked back, he saw the family preparation period had made a deep impression on him.

Since congregational worship is so important in the body of Christ, should we not expect believers to prepare themselves? Some people reserve their Saturday evenings as quiet family times in anticipation of Sunday worship. That seems encouraging and proper. Others rise early on Sunday morning for meditation and reflection. Such personal preparation means that we enter worship services having divested ourselves of the peripheral issues swirling around us. Our minds have been cleared of the distractions that would inhibit our worship so we can focus our attention on God.

This process of preparation is what Webber calls "centering." That term "refers to the intentional focus of our inner person . . . on God, the Father, the Son, and the Holy Spirit."[8] We all need to center ourselves before God as we approach worship. Though each person must do that personally, it is a process that can be taught and encouraged.

Perhaps each Sunday school teacher, as a minimum concession to teaching about preparation for worship, could stop teaching 5 minutes early and lead the class in a short time of quiet meditation and prayer.

We have said several times in this book that worship is a priority of our mission. That being true, all ministries of the church should in some way lead us to God to adore Him. We must involve the Sunday school in that pursuit.

Tozer said worship is "the missing jewel of the church." Unfortunately for many of us, our worship is like a diamond in the rough. We need help to take our stone, cut and polish it, and allow it to become the jewel it was intended to be. The Sunday school can be a primary means, used by the Holy Spirit, to turn our worship into a precious jewel.

NOTES

[1] Robert E. Webber, *Worship Is a Verb* (Waco, TX: Word Books, 1985), p. 21.

[2] David Watson, *I Believe in Evangelism* (Grand Rapids: Wm. B. Eerdmans Publishing Co., 1977), p. 173.

[3] George H. Mallone, *Furnace of Renewal* (Downers Grove, IL: InterVarsity Press, 1981), p. 51.

[4] Ibid, p. 52.

[5] Webber, p. 131.

[6] Robert Schmidgall, "Worship: Preparing Yourself and Your Congregation," *Leadership Journal,* Summer 1981, Vol. II, No. 3, p. 114.

[7] Webber, p. 94.

[8] Ibid, p. 102.

8

Fellowship and Mission

The Church spoken of in the Bible is people. It is not buildings and properties; it is not an organization. It is an organism, made up of living, breathing human beings. The Church is not, however, just any group of people. The Church is people with a particular identity. They are a chosen people, a royal priesthood, a holy nation, a people belonging to God, called out by Him from the world (Exodus 19:5,6; 1 Peter 2:9). Over the years, these people have been called many things: *brethren, believers, saints, elect, disciples, Christians,* and *those of the Way.* Perhaps the best description is simply the *body of Christ.*

What those in the Church are called is not so important as why they are called. The people who make up Christ's church have been chosen for a purpose. They have a mission.

How well they fulfill their mission is directly related to the quality of their life together. Christians are supposed to reflect a distinct quality of fellowship and community with one another. A unique *oneness* should mark the people of God, convincing the secular world that they are indeed disciples of Christ (John 13:34,35).

Howard Snyder, writing in *Community of the King,* maintains that "community is essential, for where it is lacking, and where there are no working structures to nourish it, the leaven becomes inactive and the salt loses its savor."[1]

God's people must understand and live out what it means to be in fellowship with one another in order for the church's mission to be accomplished as it should.

That may sound easy, but closer analysis reveals a disturbing truth. Far too many Christians have no real understanding of what authentic, Biblical fellowship means. Fellowship has been reduced to little more than 5 minutes of shaking hands on Sunday morning, an after-service snack at a local restaurant, or attending a men's or ladies' breakfast.

Though *fellowship* is one of the most often used words in the church, the image most people have of it is inaccurate. Fellowship is never something casual, trite, or purely social. In the New Testament, fellowship has a rich, deep meaning we need to rediscover. Few truths are more ignored and misunderstood than the meaning of Christian fellowship.

Aspects of Fellowship

Ultimately, the effectiveness of our mission as the church is tied to the success with which we live out real fellowship in the body of Christ. To understand this point, we must first define what we mean by fellowship. It has to do with the quality and conduct of the relationships that exist among people in the church. Those relationships have several identifiable marks.

1. *The people of God should relate to one another in unity.* This unity is based on the work of God through Jesus Christ. All Christian believers are fellow citizens, joint heirs and mutual partakers of the promise of God. The church is a family. The people are the children of God.

That is not to say that the oneness and unity we have in Christian fellowship means uniformity. God has made each individual unique, but in a beautiful paradox, His Spirit takes each unique person and makes him one with his brother and sister in Christ.

Christian fellowship takes place among people in whom the barriers of the world have been abolished. Among Christians no such thing as race, nationality, slavery, freedom, gender, youth, or old age is to exist. Christ did away with such distinctions. Pride and prejudice have no place among us. In Christ all believers have equal standing.

The unity we have in fellowship is a matter of utmost importance to Christ. In His only recorded prayer for the future

Church, Jesus appealed to the Father that His followers would all be one and that their oneness would be of the same quality as that which exists between Him and the Father (John 17:20,21).

Paul used the analogy of the human body to describe the function of the Church in mission. Each person, like separate parts of the body, has a distinct and important part to play. Every part, responding to the head, working toward the same purpose, presents a picture of health and stability. And, of course, when arms, legs, eyes, and ears work toward separate ends, they present the image of a retarded or spastic body.

Unity is the quality of fellowship that is fundamental to accomplishing our mission. No church with disunity in its ranks will ever achieve its purpose.

2. *The people of God should provide a mutual support group for one another.* This is achieved in intimate, caring relationships.

The first thing God described as "not good" was Adam's loneliness (Genesis 2:18). Most theologians observe a principle in this text that applies to relationships beyond marriage. Aloneness is not God's will for His people. Humans were created gregarious. Those who say they want to be left completely alone are not psychologically well. A healthy condition of life is to want to be with others in significant relationships. People need mutual fellowship; that is how God created them.

Perhaps the most destabilizing thing in our culture today is not fear of nuclear holocaust or international terrorism. Rather, it is the continual erosion of meaningful relationships. In our increasingly technological society, the value of the individual continues to diminish. It is a sad and ironic observation that so many people rub shoulders with masses of other people, yet feel so utterly alone. In a sense, large crowds increase loneliness rather than cure it.

God has created people with the desire to know and be known by others. People need to be loved and they need to love. Such things simply cannot happen in large masses of people. It is true that we get lost in crowds—not just physically but psychologically as well.

The people of God are intended to function like a family. The family unit is a small primary center for growth, development, and maturity. Growth takes place in the mix of relationships in both the nuclear family and the extended family: parents, children, aunts, uncles, grandparents, and cousins. All those relationships provide a caring context for loving and growing. That is why the only child may be at a loss at times. Though he has the relationships of the extended family, in his nuclear family he has no sibling relationships, which could make a valuable contribution to his maturation process.

Christians also need a mix of family relationships. The believer who acts like an only child suffers by absenting himself from the relationships he needs the most. Taking a "Lone Ranger" approach to church—coming with no real desire or intention to be in relationship with others—has devastating consequences.

Thus, the goal must be to incorporate all of God's people into fellowship in such a way that they experience meaningful and significant relationships with others. But what kind of relationships are we speaking of?

The Bible makes some very bold and, to the secular mind, outrageous claims about friendship among believers. It suggests that believers should be so close to one another that they can bear one another's burdens. If one member of the body suffers, all are supposed to identify with the pain and respond. If one member rejoices, the others are to share in the party! Christians are to experience such depth of caring that they can be open and trusting enough to confess their faults to one another. In our society, that is radical teaching!

Yet it is precisely that sort of caring that people need and desire most. We all need a place where we can be cared for and strengthened. We all need trusted friends with whom to share our lives. Christian fellowship must build those attitudes, or our fellowship will fall short of the Biblical expectations.

Bruce Larson tells the story of serving a church during his

seminary days in which fellowship consisted of monthly men's and women's meetings. One week, he heard about a teenage girl in the congregation who had moved away because she was pregnant. He asked if he could visit her. He was told that he (the minister) was the last person she wanted to see. He continues,

> Suddenly it hit me: That's what's wrong with the church in our time. It's the place you go when you put on your best clothes; you sit in Sunday school, you worship, you have a potluck dinner together, but you don't bring your life! You leave behind all your pain, your brokenness, your hopes, even your joys.[2]

Notice that all the things he mentioned as not being present are just what the Bible tells us we should be sharing.

Remember that Jesus commanded believers to love one another. So in Biblical terms, building intimacy and close friendship is not optional. Jesus has commanded us to build what we need most. Because we all share together the common work of Christ in our lives we already have the basis for deep friendship.

When, as a Christian, I find other brothers and sisters with whom I can share the depth of my life, I receive one of the most precious gifts God has ever given mankind.

In this day of large highly organized churches, we must remember that close Christian fellowship emerges best out of the small group. Ironically, the church is more institutionalized than ever at just the time people most want fellowship.

To advocate doing away with large churches is simplistic—as well as unbiblical. The proper response is for large churches to work diligently to ensure the presence of small fellowship groups within their congregations.

3. *The people of God must encourage one another to achieve spiritual growth and do good works.* Hebrews 10:23-25 contains the principle here. We should "consider how we may spur one another on toward love and good deeds" (v. 24). Our fellowship

can be the most productive and effective means of encouraging one another toward achieving our mission.

It is no accident that some of the most world-shaking movements in church history had their beginnings in small-group fellowships. Among them was the English Reformation that began out of the White Horse Inn group, a number of men who met for fellowship and to study Erasmus' translation of the Scriptures.[3] Methodism began with the Holy Club at Oxford. Much of our modern missions efforts can be traced to the "haystack group," a dedicated group of young men who began to meet regularly to plan for missions. Today the world's largest church, in Seoul, South Korea, is built on the strength of small cell groups. Let us not forget that Jesus invested in a small group of 12 men, 11 of whom went on to turn the world upside down.

These small groups were made up of friends, committed to Christ, who shared the common goal of doing all they could to accomplish their mission for Jesus. They encouraged one another. They dreamed together. They prayed and cried together.

The goal of stimulating one another to do good deeds is in keeping with our being in a priesthood of believers. The Bible clearly teaches that each of us is our brother's keeper. It is our responsibility to help our brothers and sisters please God with their lives.

In that respect, one of the best things that can happen in Christian fellowship is the idea of accountability. Everyone needs someone he trusts and with whom he can share his spiritual pilgrimage and growth. We need someone with whom we can be totally honest and know that we will be loved and cared for. We need loving friends who will tell us the truth about ourselves. Paul hints at this in Ephesians 5:21 where he tells believers to be mutually submitted to one another out of reverence for Christ.

It is tragic when the body of Christ allows members to seemingly remain disconnected, achieving no growth in their lives and having no one concerned enough to confront them in a loving, caring way. Such an attitude does not conform to the idea of being our brother's keeper.

Our fellowship must reflect encouragement and affirmation. It should promote worth and humanity in people. True fellowship recognizes the image of God in others. It builds friendships that will challenge one another to attempt great things in the kingdom of God.

In close, mutual fellowship we can work out true Christianity without facades. At least that should be happening. Whether it actually does depends on the degree of trust and love evident among the believers.

Before Christianity is *religion* it is *relationship:* first with Christ, then with one another. In that relationship, we should be free to be honest about ourselves, to accept and love one another, and to encourage one another to obediently respond to the call of Christ.

In this way, we are truly different from the world. Secular relationships often are cold, filled with distrust, and marked by jealousy, disregard, and criticism. The fellowship of the saints should model the opposite.

True Christian fellowship expresses itself positively, building one another up in a display of kindness, patience, forgiveness, hospitality, service, comfort, and thanks.

Fellowship was so deep in the Jerusalem church that it was expressed in the sharing of all things among the saints (see Acts 2:44 and 4:32). It was a fellowship of giving and receiving not just money but devotion, commitment, time, concern, listening, and support. Our present fellowship rarely approaches the depth described in the Bible.

We must take our fellowship more seriously. We still have all things in common in Christ, even though we may not practically demonstrate it.

4. *The people of God must serve together.* We must work in unison to complete the mission that has been given to the Church.

John Stott wrote,

> Fellowship is more than what we share "in" together. It is also what we share "out" together... our common service. The church is a great fellowship of fishers of men. Note Paul's use of fellowship in Galatians 2:9 where he describes how the Jerusalem apostles—James, Peter, and John—gave to him and Barnabas the right hand of fellowship. What did that symbolize? It was a token of partnership in mission.[4]

Remember that we are an army. We train together, live together, receive our orders from the same source, and fight against a common foe.

When an army goes to battle, each soldier needs to know he can trust his comrades. Such confidence results from the fellowship they build in their training and life experiences. Likewise, when believers experience true fellowship they can go boldly to battle, knowing their brothers and sisters march beside them.

A believer left alone to contemplate the mission of the church and his particular part in that plan can easily be overwhelmed at the enormousness of the task. But put that same person in a larger group of excited, caring people committed to the same cause, and great confidence will grow. What seems impossible alone can be attainable together. Thus, Christian fellowship provides the relational basis upon which our mission is accomplished.

In this world, Christians have always been a minority, yet they are challenged to tell *everyone* about Jesus. It seems like an impossible task for a minority. But if that minority is trained well, empowered supernaturally, strengthened by the fellowship of its comrades, and willing to go, the task can be accomplished.

The simple truth of that statement has often been demonstrated in an object lesson using toothpicks. If you take one toothpick and bend it in the middle, it will snap. However, if you put 20 toothpicks together and try to bend them, nothing will happen. Alone, the toothpick is fragile, but together with other toothpicks, it takes on strength and can resist enormous pressure. Such is the critical importance of working together with fellow Christians.

Consider another important truth. We live in an age of easy-believism. Some theologies in our culture teach Christians they need never suffer or be in want. Such philosophies simply deny the human condition and place man in a near-heavenly state.

Yet the Bible reminds us that we are still very human and susceptible to the human condition (see 2 Corinthians 4). As we work to accomplish our mission, brothers and sisters may be wounded. They may go through difficult times and have needs. Genuine fellowship requires that we be there to help them at such times.

It is no coincidence that great bravery emerges in wartime. I have an image from the 1960s of a young GI carrying a wounded friend to a waiting helicopter while bullets fly around him. Why do men risk their lives for others? They do so because they care and love. They sense a deep duty and devotion to their fellowmen, especially their comrades-in-arms.

The people of God must serve together during the rough times as well as the good. We must help a wounded brother, even at great personal risk. Jesus is our example in this. He said, "Greater love has no one than this, that one lay down his life for his friends" (John 15:13, NASB). Though speaking of himself, He had just made the point that the servanthood He modeled was expected of all those who would follow Him (John 13:1-17).

If I have real fellowship with my fellow Christians, I will never leave a wounded brother unattended. My mission includes serving those inside as well as outside the household of faith.

5. *The fellowship of God's people, in itself, is a fundamental component of our mission.* When the secular world looks at Christians, if it sees a loving community, this will be a powerful witness the Holy Spirit can use to draw the observer to Christ. This is the point of John 13:34,35.

Jesus said that believers should love one another as He loved them. How did He love them? He laid down His life for them.

We love one another as He loved when we lay down our lives and agendas for our brothers and sisters. That means we stop being selfish and live our lives reaching out to others. Jesus also said when men see love among believers, they will immediately recognize those people as Christians.

Dr. Francis Schaeffer commented on John 13:34,35 in his book *The Mark of the Christian*.[5] He said that implicit in this passage is the world's right to judge whether people who profess Jesus Christ truly belong to Him. The basis of the judgment is the degree of sacrificial love present among them. If secular men see Christians laying down their lives as Jesus did, they can say, "Yes, these people are Christians." But if the love is not present, they will say, "These people aren't really Christians!"

It is a sobering thought. Fellowship is not an option but an absolute imperative. We must remember that people are observing us at all times. They are making judgments about whether we are truly followers of Christ. Our responsibility is to show them what we are by the degree of loving fellowship we display.

Sunday School as a Center for Fellowship

We have previously said that small groups facilitate fellowship. No ministry in the church uses small groups more effectively than the Sunday school. The goal must be to make each class a place where fellowship is encouraged and demonstrated, with special emphasis on the adult classes.

Howard Snyder reminds us that our fellowship is brought about by the Holy Spirit. It is a gift from the Spirit. The church creates the environment in which the Spirit works to bring our fellowship into operation.

If Snyder is right, then we must deliberately gather the church together for the purpose of experiencing fellowship. The Sunday school class can be an ideal setting for this if we will do a few simple things.

1. *Remember the class is a place for people to learn, grow,*

and experience fellowship together. It is not for the teacher only. If the teacher lectures for 50 minutes with no opportunity for interaction among the people, fellowship will never develop. If, however, the teacher values each individual and determines to have each person share, then the seeds of fellowship will be sown.

2. *Structure the class to allow "every-person" participation.* Attention should be given to introducing new people, getting to know them, and encouraging one or more class members to befriend them. The teaching should utilize involvement learning methods such as small groups, discussions, and questions and answers. This not only results in better teaching, but also builds Christian community. As people share, they get to know and care about one another.

The class atmosphere should be open and accepting. Letting people know they will be loved and accepted regardless of what they share is important.

3. *Always follow up on absentees.* We've heard it all our lives in Sunday school, but it is fundamental. People need to know they are genuinely loved and not being taken for granted. If they are absent, nothing speaks louder about the quality of fellowship than people calling, writing a card, or making a personal visit. Such small tokens can speak volumes about Christian love.

4. *Have the members meet besides as a class.* Though the class structure may begin and promote fellowship, it will soon become too confining as fellowship grows. It is important to meet together in other settings: homes, socials, service projects, schools, and the like. People need to get to know one another in more natural settings as they deepen their relationships. This will result in more knowledge of one another, which will create greater caring and response.

Home fellowship is as old as the church. Acts 2:42-46 describes it. Besides going to the temple together, the believers met in their homes. They prayed together and shared meals. Their fellowship was built around the normal flow of their lives.

It had its beginning in the work of Christ and then naturally expressed itself in common daily living.

John Wesley echoed this same concept when he addressed a gathering on April 25, 1742:

> I appointed several earnest and sensible men to meet me, to whom I showed the great difficulty I had long found of knowing the people who desired to be under my care. After much discourse, they all agreed there could be no better way to come to a sure, thorough knowledge of each person than to divide them into classes, like those at Bristol, under the inspection of those in whom I could most confide. This was the origin of our classes at London, for which I can never sufficiently praise God, the unspeakable usefulness of the institution having ever since been more and more manifest.[6]

The Sunday school must do something else of importance in order to fellowship. Just as leaders must ensure the doctrinal soundness of the teaching staff, great care must be taken to choose Sunday school teachers who can encourage fellowship.

Sunday school teachers must be friendly, outgoing, caring, and good communicators. They need good "people skills" because they will facilitate the quality of fellowship that arises in their classes.

If teachers recognize the importance of fellowship, they will conduct the class in such a way as to attain it. If they fail to recognize the importance of fellowship, they may inadvertently hinder its development.

A teacher who desires to build fellowship will arrive early for class and stay late. He or she will seek out people and talk with them. The teaching and interaction will be people-oriented and people's needs will receive priority attention.

How the teacher instructs can either promote or destroy fellowship. If the teacher talks for the entire period, never allowing anyone to speak, he is robbing people of self-esteem. The message conveyed is that only the teacher has anything useful to contribute; everyone else is in need and should listen. However, if the teacher will simply ask a question, he will create a wonderful dynamic in the class. First, he is affirming that others have something important to contribute and that he is not the only person of importance in the classroom. Further, as people are allowed to provide answers and information, their self-worth is built up. Just the simple act of letting others speak allows fellowship to be introduced. The teacher controls whether or not that happens.

With very little effort from a few key people, the Sunday school can become the dynamic center for fellowship in the church. Once fellowship begins, it gains momentum and life of its own. The consequences will be people who love one another, who encourage one another, and who work together to accomplish the mission of the church.

Erich Fromm wrote,

> A man sits in front of a bad television program and doesn't know that he is bored; he joins the rat race of commerce, where personal worth is measured in terms of market values, and is not aware of his anxiety. Ulcers speak louder than words. Theologians and philosophers have been saying for a century that God is dead, but what we confront now is the possibility that man is dead, transformed into a thing, a producer, a consumer, an idolater of other things.[7]

Genuine Biblical fellowship can make man alive again!

NOTES

[1] Howard A. Snyder, *Community of the King* (Downers Grove, IL: Inter-Varsity Press, 1977), p. 58.

[2] Bruce Larson, "None of Us Are Sinners Emeritus," *Leadership Journal,* Fall 1984, Vol. V, No. 4, p. 14.

[3] John R. W. Stott, *One People* (Old Tappan, NJ: Fleming H. Revell Company, 1968), pp. 81,82.

[4] Ibid., p.87,88.

[5] Francis A. Schaeffer, *The Mark of the Christian* (Downers Grove, IL: Inter-Varsity Press, 1970), pp. 16-18.

[6] Howard A. Snyder, *The Problem of Wineskins* (Downers Grove, IL: Inter-Varsity Press, 1975), p. 174.

[7] Erich Fromm, *Leadership,* Fall 1984, Vol. V, No. 4, p. 78.

9

Leadership and Mission

At times in the past, tribes and nations have attempted to settle disputes in a rather novel way: resorting to a champion to fight for the entire group. The warring tribes would meet at some designated location and two champions, each representing a side, would engage in combat while the larger groups observed. It was usually winner-take-all. The champion who prevailed claimed the victory, which included subjugating the losing population and other spoils of war.

(The theory is not all bad. If there is going to be bloodshed, better one man's than hundreds'. Furthermore, if you pick your best man, his chances represent your greatest probability of success. Of course, the other side does the same.)

However, stakes were equally high. If the champion lost, his whole nation went into captivity. In fact, the risks in this style of combat were so great that no nation uses the system today.

Many contemporary evangelical/Pentecostal churches, without realizing it, seem to employ this old strategy in the spiritual battles they fight. The churches are at war with the forces of darkness. Rather than mobilizing all the believers into the active service of the army, a champion is chosen to fight the battle alone. More often than not, he is the pastor, and he is chosen by default.

The way the church employs this type of combat, however, differs in two significant ways: First, rather than watching and rooting for the champion, believers tend to take off to do their own thing, and the pastor battles alone. Second, the forces of darkness, rather than choosing a champion, usually throw their entire army into the conflict. It doesn't sound fair, does it? It is certainly not the way the Bible expects us to wage spiritual warfare.

One of the most significant and common problems faced by churches is overworked leaders and underused laity. It is a problem that must be solved if the church is ever to accomplish its mission.

John Palmer describes the situation in his book *Equipping for Ministry*. He writes,

> In too many churches today, the pastor and the other "professional clergy" are seen as The Ministers. They are expected to carry out the "ministry of the church." They take care of the visitation, counseling, preaching, organizing, driving the young people to a retreat, planning the music, etc. What happens as a result? They wear themselves out, burn themselves out, and become largely ineffective. The pastor's family also suffers as a result of the stress the pastor feels. Meanwhile, on the sidelines wait scores of people who need to experience the joy of serving the Lord. Not only do they need to serve, they *want* to serve. They are saying, "Give me an opportunity. Just show me how."[1]

Palmer is correct. We are in the midst of a great renewal of lay interest in church involvement.

In the February 3, 1984, edition of *Christianity Today*, Dr. Robert Johnson wrote an article titled "What Is the Major Shift in Theological Focus?" His article said that the 1950s was the decade of emphasis on Christology. The 1960s emphasized God the Father and the nature of the Church. The 1970s focused on the nature and ministry of the Holy Spirit. It is his conviction that the 1980s' main theological thrust is about God's people. This is borne out by training such as this, emphasizing the laity and their place in Christ's kingdom.

The news is good. We may be able to rediscover the reality of body ministry. However, we must have a plan, a strategy, for training this emerging army for their mission.

It is not the intent of this book to deal at length with equipping saints for service. That has been done in *Equipping for*

Leadership and Mission 109

Ministry. However, we must consider the role of leadership as it relates to the church's mission, especially preparing people for service.

Leadership must commit itself to the Biblical-theological teaching about the church. In a previous chapter dealing with doctrine, we pointed to the imperative of having a Biblical base for mission. The Bible offers a pattern for the church that, if followed, would involve all believers in mission and radically intensify the process of evanglizing the world.

Part of the Biblical plan deals with the role of leadership. Ephesians 4:11-16 teaches that the Lord gives the church leaders whose primary responsibility is to train believers to serve. This teaching is not found only in Ephesians. Rather, it is part of an extensive theology of training that runs through the Scriptures. God's Word holds numerous examples of training: Moses in Pharaoh's court, Samuel in Eli's house, Elisha under Elijah, the tribe of Levi before the other tribes, Jesus and His disciples, Paul's letters to Timothy and Titus. The list could be expanded.

Furthermore, the Bible also contains much teaching about the importance of training. Fathers are commanded to teach their children (Deuteronomy 6:7; Proverbs 22:6). The kings, judges, and priests were commanded to teach the people to obey God.

In two classic texts, believers are commanded to train: (1) 2 Timothy 2:15 instructs Christians to study to gain divine approval and an ability to correctly handle God's Word, and (2) Matthew 28:19,20 includes the challenge to teach new converts to obey all Christ commanded.

The whole idea of a discipling, Christian education ministry is built on the need to teach people what it means to be a Christian and live effectively in the Kingdom.

The ability to train and teach is a Biblical prerequisite for leadership in the church. The Bible teaches that leaders are given to supervise and be responsible for training ministries. In 2 Timothy 2:2, Paul writes, "The things you have heard me say in the presence of many witnesses entrust to reliable men who will also be qualified to teach others."

The Bible not only contains examples of people in training and instructions to do the same, it also offers models of where such training may take place.

In the Old Testament, the basic unit for teaching about God was the family. Over time, that expanded to include the synagogue as a center of worship and instruction.

The Early Church adopted that idea, redefining it into what we know as the church. In fact, the church became such an important center for training that for hundreds of years it was the only center for formal education.

To ignore the Christian education ministry is to reject the overwhelming Biblical mandate to support it. Nevertheless, in many churches today it is easy to find dynamic worship, strong fellowship, and good outreach, but difficult to find an exciting Christian education program.

Why Is Training So Important to the Church's Mission?

Training is vital because it propagates the faith. It has been often said that the church is only one generation from extinction at any time. What does that mean? Simply, it means that every generation must tell the gospel to the next one and lead them to Christ. The moment we stop teaching our children, the church will be mortally wounded. We must pass the gospel along to our children and all those who are new believers. We must teach them to teach their children. That builds continuity and ensures that the faith will go on even after the present generation passes.

Training is important because it creates a unity of purpose. When we train in the church, we are preparing God's people for the same task. We all share the same goal and train to accomplish it. All Christians in the world celebrate their oneness in the celebration of Communion. In a very real sense, Christians also share their oneness in the mission they have to accomplish. Christ's Great Commission is the same for all believers.

Christians are a minority in the world. That has always been true and remains so today. We are outnumbered by nonbelievers, but that does not change our mission of evangelizing the world. How can we do it? By worshiping God, appealing to His power, and being unified as a spiritual army.

In the first century, the Roman army had a crack group of soldiers called the *kustodias*. They were a small unit of men who were specially trained for intense combat and difficult assignments. It was written that a squad of 12 *kustodias* could defend against hundreds of enemy soldiers. They were each trained to protect 1 square yard of land against an oncoming army. These soldiers had brave hearts, strong bodies, single-minded purpose, and total trust in one another. It was soldiers of this caliber who often made it possible for the Roman army to defeat enemy armies several times their size.

Likewise, when Christians are trained for service, when they are brave in the Spirit, trust one another, and have a single-minded purpose, they can easily defeat the enemies around them because they have the Holy Spirit's help to enable and equip them.

No church will ever accomplish its mission if its members head off in dozens of different directions without purpose or vision. God gives leaders to establish the plan and train the army for the battle. A unified army leads to success.

Training builds confidence in people. The church is the largest volunteer community in the world. Many people who offer themselves in service to the church have no prior experience or knowledge of the areas in which they will serve. What are leaders to do with such people? We can reject their service or we can place them in service without training or knowledge, in which case they will probably fail. Or we can take these willing people and train them to understand and practice their ministry and then assign them. They will invariably succeed. Why? Because after they are trained, they know what to do and why. They go boldly into service.

A young man who felt God was calling him into his church's bus ministry offered his service to the pastor. The pastor, desperately seeking bus workers, rejoiced that God had called the young man. Without hesitation, he offered the young man the keys to the buses and a list of names of other people who might be willing to assist.

After several weeks in which little or nothing was done, the pastor called the young man to his office and inquired. The young man said he had no idea what to do or how to start. The pastor took the keys and began looking for someone else. At the same time, the pastor typed the young man as misguided and lazy. Everybody lost.

What went wrong in this story? Did God really speak to the young man? Yes. Was he right in going to the pastor to volunteer? Yes. Was the pastor right in sending him immediately into service? No.

The pastor thrust the man into a position for which he was unprepared. By so doing, he inadvertently set the young man up for failure.

How could events have been changed? The pastor could have placed the young man under someone's supervision for training. After a period of time for learning and practicing, the young man could have been assigned. Following this procedure, he probably would have been very successful. Everyone would have won and the kingdom of God would have benefited.

Leaders should memorize the following two-part equation:

Training (knowledge and experience) = Confidence

Zeal + Training = Success

Training creates a task-oriented Christian education ministry. We are training people for a definite purpose: Christ's mission. Therefore, all we do in Christian education must be structured with that goal in mind. We are not educating just to nurture believers. We are educating to equip believers to do something specific. Training for mission makes the church extroverted and dynamic.

In this context, Christian education is never seen as an end in itself, but as a means to a greater end, namely loving God and sharing Him with the entire world. Christian education ministries will be dynamic and productive only as they identify their clear purpose of equipping people for mission.

The Attitudes of Leaders Toward Training

We have said that training is a Biblical necessity for accomplishing the church's mission. The responsibility to train rests with those whom God has given to the Church for that purpose. Leaders must have an effective strategy for training, but first they must have right attitudes. Let us examine three attitudes of leadership that are crucial to the success of training for mission.

1. *Leaders, especially pastors, must abandon the notion of a dichotomy between clergy and laity.* Using our modern definitions, we would have to say that Christianity began as a lay movement. Consider the picture Robert B. Munger paints in an article titled "Training the Laity for Ministry":

> Suppose that you were to learn that a new religious movement had arisen in Southern California under the leadership of a carpenter from East Los Angeles, who had "turned on" some fishermen from San Pedro, an internal revenue agent and a few "hard-hats." How seriously would you take the religion? Christianity, in its beginnings, was a lay movement. Later on, the early church would be joined by a number of priests (Acts 6:7) and a few highly educated professionals like Stephen and Saul of Tarsus. But they were the exception and not the rule (1 Corinthians 1:26-28). For the most part, the ministry and missionary activity was carried on by non-professionals, ordinary men and women involved in secular work.[2]

It was to these common people that Christ gave gifts with which to minister. The Church has always been, and should be today, one people.

Laity comes from a Greek word *(laikos)* denoting those who belong to the *laos,* or chosen people of God. All who receive Jesus as Saviour and Lord make up the *laos.* The laity make up the Church.

It was not until after the first century, when the Greco-Roman influence filtered into the church, that a difference emerged between the laity and the *kleros* (from which we get the word *clergy*), those who were trained in religious affairs and had power to act. *Laos* was redefined and took on the idea of non-trained, uneducated people.

The consequences of this ecclesiastical evolution was a sharp division between professionally trained and powerful leaders on one hand, and the masses of uneducated, submissive laity on the other.

That is a departure from the Biblical idea. According to Kenneth Van Wyk, the word *kleros,* when it refers to the church in the New Testament, designates all those who share the inheritance of God's redemption and glory. The New Testament implies nothing of a separate, powerful class of religious professionals called clergy.

It was a desire to return to the Biblical pattern that helped spur the Protestant Reformation. Martin Luther sought to define and experience a priesthood of all believers, who had personal access to God and could minister in His name.

Leaders must acknowledge that we are all one body. Clergy and laity share common ministry. Though our function may differ, our mission is the same. The pastor and people together are responsible for ministry. The clergy must boldly take the lead in teaching the laity of their importance and equipping them to minister.

More than anything else, discovering this Biblical truth would cure much of the burnout that is so rampant among the clergy.

A word of caution should be mentioned here. Human beings have a tendency to swing from one extreme to another, rather than balance themselves. This is no less true in the church. As we experience this awesome rediscovery of lay ministry, it is tempting for people to swing from the extreme of "no laity, all clergy" to "all laity, no clergy." Some people have plunged into their newfound ministry and want to throw out altogether the idea of a professional clergy.

Neither extreme is valid. The need for professional clergy

remains. However, they are to be primarily pastor-teachers. The pastor's preaching, counseling, administration, and all other efforts must take on the goal of equipping others.

2. *Leaders must be disciplers.* If we are going to evangelize the world, it will require a total effort from all believers. Leaders must come to grips with the challenge of training every Christian for mission. It can be done, but for many leaders it will require a reorientation of their methods and priorities. We have no choice. What we need is a plan. Consider how Jesus went about the task of training some very average lay people.

a. *He was willing to spend personal time with them.* He walked and talked with them. He shared His life with these men, using life situations to teach and model ministry. The most profound impact one person can have on another occurs in a significant relationship. When I invest my life in another, that bond seals all I teach and model.

I discovered the reality of this when a man in our congregation lost his job. While waiting for new employment to develop, he spent too much time at home with too little to do. He soon became depressed and anxious.

To help him, I invited him to accompany me while I visited, taught, and conducted various other ministries. As we were together, he observed how I approached ministry. We had opportunities to discuss, share dreams and goals, deal with questions, and enjoy fellowship. Spending the time together affected both our lives. That was Jesus' preferred method of discipling others.

b. *Jesus taught the Word of God.* There is no substitute for providing our people with a solid Biblical basis for all they do. We must be good teachers. It is no accident that Ephesians 4 says the Lord gives pastor/teachers.

c. *Jesus took teaching one important step further.* He not only taught them the Word of God, He showed them how to live it. He provided a lab experience for them and modeled ministry for them to observe.

Educational psychologists have emphasized the value of modeling as a teaching tool. Nothing has as powerful an impact on a student as what is called the use of self, that is, using oneself as a teaching aid.

Certainly this is what Paul was doing when he encouraged others to follow his example (Philippians 3:17). Children learn more from what they observe their parents doing than from what parents say. The principle holds true in almost every relationship. We teach more by our example than by any other means.

d. *Jesus was willing to trust His disciples with responsibility.* This reminds us of our prior discussion. When it comes to ministry, clergy and laity must be undivided. Only our functions are different. The clergy must take the initiative and acknowledge that lay people can be trusted with important ministries. Any other attitude reflects a prejudice for which we leaders should repent. Jesus took simple fishermen—just plain, common folk—and entrusted them with the commission to evangelize the entire world.

e. *Jesus empowered His disciples.* In His last discourse, He promised to send the Holy Spirit to remind them of all He had taught and to be their Comforter. *Comforter* comes from two Latin words, *com,* meaning "with," and *forte,* meaning "strength." The Holy Spirit, our Comforter, is the One who comes to us with strength.

Why do we need His strength? We cannot accomplish our mission alone. We are too weak. With the Holy Spirit, we can do all things.

Jesus recognized this and gave His disciples what they needed to succeed. We must help those we train to receive the Holy Spirit. Empowered by the Holy Spirit, the army of God will not fail.

f. *Jesus promised He would never leave them as they set out in mission.* He assured them that as they went into the world to make disciples, baptize, and teach, He would be with them always with all power and authority. Few promises in the Scriptures could mean more to us than that. Why?

Because at times accepting our mission is risky and involves personal suffering. As we bear the cross with Jesus, it may mean suffering with Him in persecution. For some of our brothers and sisters in mission it means death. The mission of the church is not trite. It is a life and death matter.

When I am being persecuted or suffering, knowing that Christ was persecuted, that He overcame, and that He is with me in the midst of it makes the difference.

3. *Leaders must commit themselves to spend their time doing the things that matter most.* The pastor-teacher is given to the church to equip believers for service. As an elder, he is to devote himself to prayer and the Word of God. He is, first and foremost, to be a spiritual leader.

Accomplishing these tasks requires a strict adherence to proper priorities. More often than not, a pastor's quality time is eroded by secondary administrative matters, unnecessary phone calls, committee meetings, and a host of other activities that threaten to occupy all his waking hours.

Leaders must work with the attitude that they are Biblically called for very specific purposes and nothing can be more important than doing these things well.

Pastors must remind themselves that they are not called to do the church's ministry for it. Rather, they are called to train the people to do the ministry.

To learn the strategies for equipping believers for ministry, refer to the book *Equipping for Ministry*. It is enough here to say that until leadership recognizes the importance of lay training for mission, we will never succeed. In most of our churches we have vast armies of untapped people in the pews waiting to be mobilized into service. That is the challenge of leadership.

Robert Munger tells this story.

> In 1962 it was my privilege to hear the late missionary-theologian Hendrik Kraemer deliver a series of addresses in Beirut, Lebanon, in which he shared some of the material incorporated in his book *The Theology of the Laity*. He made the statement that the Christian church of the West was in the process of undergoing a reformation promising to be as extensive in its impact as that which occurred under Martin Luther. The church, he observed, is recover-

ing the authentic ministry of the laity that Martin Luther affirmed in the principle of the priesthood of all believers, but which in practice he was not able fully to institute. I believe he was prophetic in his judgment. The awakening of the laity to their high calling in Christ as ministers to his body and his witnesses and servants in the world, is, in the words of Robert Hudnut, stirring "The Sleeping Giant."[3]

NOTES

[1]John M. Palmer, *Equipping for Ministry* (Springfield, MO: Gospel Publishing House, 1985), p. 23.

[2]Robert B. Munger, "Training the Laity for Ministry," *Theology News and Notes,* June 1973, published by Fuller Theological Seminary, p. 1.

[3]Ibid, p. 2.

10
Method and Mission

There is a delightfully funny book called *The Official Rules*. Author Paul Dickson has compiled over 1,500 laws, rules, principles, and axioms describing everyday life. Most of us are familiar with one such example, Murphy's Law. Of course, the book is tongue-in-cheek and creates a great deal of chuckling. However, some of the laws make enough sense to read them twice.

For example, Dobbin's Law reads, "When in doubt, use a bigger hammer." What makes that law so humorous, yet so true, is that we all tend to comply with it even when we see the futility of the effort. Rather than solve the problem, we try to force things. So to speak, we reach for a bigger hammer.

In the first chapter, we recognized the problem of apparent apathy in the church. How do we solve it? How do we motivate people to involvement?

The other chapters explained our mission and its motivational influence. We defined it in relationship to several areas of the church and offered suggestions for accomplishing that mission. Most of the strategies suggested provide general direction and leave the details to the reader, allowing the local church to adapt the methods to teach people about their mission.

However, there are many established and proven ministry programs that will help people reach the goals outlined in this book.

This chapter will focus on several of those programs provided by the national Sunday School Department of the Assemblies of God, with emphasis on how they influence the church's mission.

Some people have a strong bias against using programs or materials. This feeling may be rooted in a perception that programs have been overemphasized at the expense of the work of the Holy Spirit. Perception, however, is not always truth. Probably the real source of the bias against programs is caused by a misunderstanding of their purpose.

An old axiom provides some insight:

"A program without a vision is pure drudgery;

A vision without a program is pure daydreaming."

A careful reading of the Bible reveals that God is a God of planning and order. His program for the redemption of humanity came complete with goals, strategies, resources, and timetables. Scripture nowhere suggests that God reached for a "bigger hammer" to correct some flaw or force an issue. He stayed with His program and it is still working effectively today.

A ministry that takes advantage of a program to achieve its purposes reflects order and planning. Any project must have some means for accomplishing it. The challenge is how to do it. A program can be "how to do it."

Our goal is to mobilize people for the mission of the church. For that we need a strategy, a plan of action. Sad to say, some leaders spend hours attempting to develop new programs when effective ones already exist. Let's not reinvent the wheel; let's take advantage of the work already done.

Having said this, let us focus on programs that are available in the area of discipleship training, which includes Christian education and Sunday school.

The program ministries of the Sunday School Department are primarily related to training leaders and lay persons to understand and carry out the mission of the church. In the chapter "Leadership and Mission," we referred to the strong theology of training present throughout the Bible. It is obvious that training has been, and continues to be, a primary tool for the perpetuation of the faith. God's people need to be trained for mission. From the Bible, we can make several statements about the value of training:

1. God considers training vitally important in His kingdom.
2. Training is a spiritual, theological, Biblically mandated endeavor.
3. God has gifted people to train and offer Biblical instruction.
4. God's people—the church of Jesus Christ—will function as they were intended only when attention is given to training.[1]

In light of these truths, it is unfortunate that so many churches fail to provide systematic training for their leaders, staff, and people. Perhaps training ministries are thought to be nonproductive, too difficult to administrate, or simply needless programs.

A careful analysis of growing and maturing churches reveals that, almost without exception, they have ongoing training programs throughout their various ministries.

The national Sunday School Department recognizes the importance of training and has developed training programs for the local church. Let us examine several of them and how they relate to the church's mission.

Sunday School Counselor

Perhaps the most widely used and relevant training ministry offered by the Sunday School Department is the *Sunday School Counselor,* a monthly Sunday school resource magazine.

The magazine serves three main purposes:

1. *It is motivational.* By sharing stories from local churches and inspiring articles, it reminds us of the excitement that comes to the church engaged in mission.

2. *It is informative.* Each month the *Counselor* presents valuable information about training opportunities, books, resources, people, and programs.

3. *It is instructional.* Included in each edition is material by specialists in the various fields of Christian education, offering plans, ideas, and teaching strategies.

Of constant importance to the *Counselor* is the association of Christian education with the great mission of the church, with emphasis on helping train and involve Christian educators in it.

Directions—The Way To Go for Sunday School Development

Directions defines its purpose as "a comprehensive organizational tool designed to help Sunday school leaders develop a more effective operation" by spelling out "the basic requirements and ingredients for a balanced ministry of reaching and teaching."

Directions identifies its relationship to the mission of the church as follows: "The Assemblies of God Sunday school is an evangelistic and educational agency sponsored by the church for individuals of all ages. The purpose of the . . . Sunday school is to provide the church with a ministry to reach, teach, and win the individual to Christ and to mature and train him for Christian service."[2]

Directions is an organizational plan for helping churches develop Sunday schools capable of effectively training people for mission. It includes detailed instructions in five areas: organization and administration, staffing and training, growth and evangelism, facilities and resources, and ministries.

This program provides tools for present evaluation, planning, goal setting, and follow-up. Using *Directions,* any church seriously interested in training people in mission can organize a Sunday school having that emphasis.

Sunday School Info Series

A complement to the *Directions* program is a series of informational articles called the Sunday School Info Series. These articles cover a wide variety of Sunday school related topics. They give an overview of each subject and establish its purpose. Reading them provides an important association of the topic to the Sunday school and church's mission.

Age-Level Programs

Few ministries of the church touch people at their age-level better than the Sunday school. A clear intent of age-level programs is to train individuals according to their needs and abilities to accomplish their mission as Christians.

The assumption underlying age-level ministries is simple, but profound: Every person in the church is valuable to the church's mission and can be prepared to serve well. All members—children, youth, and adults—have purpose.

The people who make up our society are changing rapidly. Thirty years ago, adults were adults; "one size fits all." However, we now know that adults go through various "change points," or transitions (young adult, mid-life, senior). Each phase produces unique problems and issues that must be addressed to help the individuals successfully pass through the change points. Adults are more complex than we previously realized.

The ages of adolescence have expanded dramatically because of two phenomena: the lower age of puberty and the fact that many teens and young adults are staying in the home longer. This presents new challenges for teaching and guiding youth.

Children are brighter and more informed than ever before. They are the children of a technological, media-centered world that challenges the methods and manner of their teaching. Yet it is still true that the easiest age-span in which to win a person to Christ is 8 to 11 years old.

It is a fact that early childhood and preschool children are more affected by their environment than thought possible in the past. Thus, training should begin earlier for them.

All these observations about various age-levels are true of people in our churches. If we are to successfully prepare people for mission, we must teach and guide them by using programs specifically designed for their age-level.

The Sunday School Department offers the following age-level handbooks designed for that purpose: *Guiding the Preschool Child, Guiding the Elementary Child, Guiding Youth,* and *Guiding Adults.* Also available is the Radiant Life Curriculum, age-level Sunday school material produced by Gospel Publishing House.

Because people do go through significant change points in their lives, it is necessary to provide programs and information directed at those transitions. For that reason the Sunday school should provide small groups, classes, and resources for single adults, senior adults, families, and others. The church must identify these groups, minister to their needs, and enlist them in the church's broader mission.

Strengthening the entire church for mission requires special attention to these groups. Recent statistics indicate that by the early 1990s, approximately 50 percent of the U.S. population will be single. The population is also getting older, for people are living longer. The breakup of the traditional American family is an issue that could fill volumes.

Offering resources, programs, and consultation, the Sunday School Department is prepared to assist local churches as they minister to special groups.

Missions Training

The Assemblies of God virtually considered itself a missions agency when it was organized and continues to provide one of the best missionary programs in the world today. Such efforts are an important part of the mission of the church. Missionary training is foundational to our faith and practice. It is central to our commission to "go and make disciples."

However, waiting to teach adults the importance of missions is costly. Such remedial training is often difficult and time-consuming. It is far better to train our children and youth about the importance of missions so when they become adults their commitment and involvement will be strong.

The Sunday School Department offers one of the best children's missions-educating programs. It is called the Boys and Girls Missionary Crusade (BGMC). To its credit, this program raises approximately $1 million dollars annually for missions work. Of even greater importance is BGMC's training purpose: teaching children about their mission to reach the world for Christ.

Specialized Programs

The Sunday School Department supplies programs to assist children's training in several other areas.

The Junior Bible Quiz program is designed to help children learn and memorize the Bible. The JBQ program introduces children to the Bible in a disciplined, structured, and challenging way. It also serves as preparation for the youth Bible quiz program.

The Sunday School Department also offers guidelines and strategy for vacation Bible school. Most people do not realize that VBS is one of the most successful outreach ministries a church can offer. As such, it is a direct expression of the church's mission.

The Sunday School Department provides assistance, direction, and materials related to extension Sunday school classes outside the traditional format. Such classes often are used for outreach as well as discipleship.

New areas of interest being developed are programs for ethnic and handicapped persons. In our society, ethnic groups make up a significant part of the population. Presently, Hispanics form the largest ethnic minority in the United States. The masses represented by these groups present a challenge to churches genuinely interested in accomplishing their mission. There must be strategies and programs for evangelizing and discipling these unique groups.

Printed Materials

Because it is primarily a support ministry for local churches, the Sunday School Department emphasizes the preparation of programs and materials that can be used by people at local levels of ministry.

This concern for preparing training materials has resulted in support resources such as

1. *The annual training book.* This book is part of the overall training program. Each year, the department commissions a book (of which this is one) about a subject related to teaching,

doctrine, evangelism, or ministry. The book comes with an instructors guide, offered to local congregations for study and practice.

2. *A certification program.* The department offers a training program for teachers and leaders, using the *Fundamentals for Sunday School Workers* books. This 52-week series is very thorough and provides instruction in Bible study, Sunday school operation, teaching methods, and doctrine. Upon completion of the FSSW, the appropriate age-level handbook, and a subscription to the *Sunday School Counselor,* individuals may receive certification as a Sunday school teacher.

3. *Workshops and other books.* The Staff Training Series comprises seminar material kits for a staff conference or retreat. They can be purchased from Gospel Publishing House.

For churches that find it necessary to offer short-term teacher training, there is *First Steps for Teachers,* a 13-week summary of the 52-week *Fundamentals for Sunday School Workers* series. It is also available from Gospel Publishing House.

Each item is intended to prepare people to better serve the church and fulfill its mission.

Curriculum

Perhaps no program of printed training materials touches more church members each week than the prepared Sunday school curriculum.

Because we staff our Christian education ministries with lay volunteers, it is imperative to provide them with curriculum to guide their teaching efforts. The printed curriculum provides a teaching guide prepared by individuals who are qualified and experienced. Printed curriculum offers doctrinal integrity, continuity, and effective instructional methods. It includes clear objectives, instructions for teaching activities, and resources. Student materials are appealing and easy to use.

The Assemblies of God provides an excellent Sunday school curriculum called Radiant Life.

In its printed form no curriculum is complete, however. Individual teachers must do something with it. The teacher is the final curriculum interpreter. That is one reason why teacher training is so important to local churches. Even the best curriculum poorly used will fail. It is important that churches train teachers for presenting the curriculum effectively.

To accomplish the mission of the Church, Christians need knowledge, zeal, and training. Training must be provided by the local church through classes and opportunities to serve. As people see what is required of them Biblically and they have opportunity to be doers of the Word, the Holy Spirit will provide the zeal they need.

People rarely accomplish their mission in the church by themselves. They need instruction and guidance. If we can provide that at the local church level, we may have the opportunity to influence the world for Christ in ways that history has never before seen.

This is a great age for education. More adults are enrolled in continuing education than the total number of students attending elementary and high schools. There is an incredible appetite for training and knowledge. We need to tap into that attitude in our churches. Most of all, we need to guide the desire for training into preparation for the Lord's service.

It is probable that in many of our churches we have people waiting to be prepared for mission and service. They represent a vast, untapped army that could be dramatically touching the world now if we would but train them.

The church is at a significant point in its history. Never before has there been such an opportunity to reach the entire world with a clear presentation of the gospel. The proliferation of Christian media makes it possible to reach most of the world with television and radio.

For those who do not have TV and radio, Christian publishing houses and distribution services provide printed resources. To this may be added the men and women who accept the call to go into remote lands and present the gospel, one-on-one if necessary.

Millions of Christians around this world are doing what they can to share Christ. Yet statistics tell us that 2 billion people have never had a clear presentation of the gospel.

We must accept the challenge to mobilize Christians around the world into service. Is it idealistic? Absolutely! Is it impossible? Who knows? Much depends on individual Christians and their accountability to Christ; on leaders and their commitment to teach, train, and guide; on the support ministries that provide programs and resources. But such a worthy and glorious goal gives us no choice but to try.

It is easy to become immobilized by the greatness of the task before us. We must resist that. We can only do what Christ requires of us personally, but we must do that well.

We should be comforted by Martin Luther, who said, "If you cannot change the world, do what you can!"

This book has been an attempt to turn our attention back to the mission of the Church, especially as it relates to Christian education and Sunday school.

Dr. D. Campbell Wyckoff, writing in *Christianity Today,* said, "Sunday school is as American as crabgrass. People, churches, theorists, have done their level best to get rid of it and yet it endures and comes back strong. For all its defects, it is the most effective agency we have ever had for Christian education."[3]

This being true, and with the urgency of the challenge to win the world for Christ, we must increase our commitment to Christian education in general and Sunday school in particular.

NOTES

[1]"The Theology of Training," Sunday School Info Series, #10, Sunday School Department of the Assemblies of God, 1445 Boonville, Springfield, MO 65802.

[2]*Directions—The Way To Go for Sunday School Development,* Sunday School Department of the Assemblies of God, 1445 Boonville, Springfield, MO 65802.

[3]"Seven Ways to Conserve Growth," Sunday School Info Series, Sunday School Department, Springfield, MO 65802.